DATE DUE

THE BRIGHT MEDUSA

M

HOWARD

MUMFORD

JONES

THE

BRIGHT

MEDUSA

The University of Illinois Press at Urbana, 1952

TO GORDON N. RAY

THE *Artist* 1 PAGE 1

The Bright Medusa originally took shape as a series of lectures delivered at the University of Illinois in March, 1952, one of the components in the remarkable Festival of Contemporary Arts held annually at that institution. To my way of thinking the arts festival shows that Vachel Lindsay, Illinois poet that he was, was right in assuming that in our republic the arts have their primary relation to the people of that republic rather than to Carnegie Hall, Fifty-Seventh Street, or academic quarterlies. This book is an examination of what happens when the arts get too far away from the general values of the culture which supports them. It is intended to be suggestive, not definitive.

Like all lectures, these discourses owe much to the attentive and kindly audiences who listened to me. The gracious invitation of the University of Illinois and the generous hospitality of Urbana are now merely memories, but they are memories rich in human affection; and as an expression of my cordial thanks to a great university this sentence is inadequate, but, alas! will have to serve.

For permission to quote, I am indebted to the following publishers: to Harcourt, Brace and Company, Inc., for Marguerite Young's poem entitled "Speculative Evening," which is from *Moderate Fable;* to Houghton Mifflin Company for excerpts from William Vaughn Moody's poems and from Willa Cather's *Song of the Lark;* and to Alfred A. Knopf, Inc., for excerpts from Miss Cather's *Youth and the Bright Medusa.*

HOWARD MUMFORD JONES

THE *Artist*

1

The literary student may be pardoned if he sometimes assents to the epigram of Napoleon that history is
a fable agreed upon. The history of literature at which
the scholar toils is a question of exactitude and docu-
mentation, the history of literature which really counts
in the publishing world is a succession of enthusiasms
and disgusts. An age arises, it writes its own books, it
grows old, its youthful successor consigns these productions to God's ash barrel, and there they remain until
some tenth successor revives their poor, lost splendors,
not as they were, but as the mirror of this new Narcissus.
The late John Livingston Lowes, in his *Convention and
Revolt in Poetry,* gave us the history of a vast systole
and diastole in the literary culture of the West, but if
any lesson was intended, it is now lost. Time has closed
over the book, and we are entranced by other masters.

The enthusiast may be right. If he does not care to work at the problem of historical imagination, or try to re-experience the shock of recognition which youth once yielded to Byron or Rochester, Marlowe or Tennyson, Villon or the goliardic poets, who can blame him? Time is short, history is long, and he is busy tossing his cap for T. S. Eliot, James Joyce, Scott Fitzgerald, or Tom Wolfe. The new master makes all things new, not only his vision of the contemporary universe, but also his vision of the past. For disciples of the prophet the seventeenth century slumbered in the arms of the Modern Language Association until some contemporary, like the prince in the fairy tale, kissed the lips of John Donne or Bishop Andrewes. Somebody else stumbled across the poems of Christopher Smart, and lo! the dead corpse of the eighteenth century sprang to life. The American wing of the literary museum was virtually unvisited until rumor went round that Melville and Hawthorne were seen there conversing with the devil. Then people rushed in to verify the tale.

In one sense no harm is done. Envy itself should be silent when an author thus revived gives pleasure to many. Nothing is gained by hinting that the figure thus exhumed is a mask, the historical trappings little more than a stage-set for a contemporary play. In another sense, however, civilization always suffers when history is curtailed and truth imperfectly understood. Whenever we take too short a view, we cripple the creative mind. Of course we do not now believe in the instant perfection of Shakespeare as the romantics did, and patient inquiry has substantiated the fact that, like any other craftsman, he had to learn his trade, adapt himself to the market, and keep an eye on the gate receipts. What we acknowledge in the case of the divine William, however, we do not always acknowledge among contemporary favorites. They seem to themselves and their admirers the first that ever burst upon a sea hitherto silent and unexplored.

But this *ultima Thule* is not altogether without report. When the modern novelist tries to make our flesh creep with his decayed Southern plantation houses, suffering females, and unnatural crimes, we have but to translate the plantation into a ruined castle, rechristen the female, Matilda, shift the adjectives slightly, and we are back with that old favorite, the Gothic romance, in our hands. Bitter and outraged young men in the modern military novel have a curious family resemblance to the bitter and outraged young men of Byron, Stendhal, Goethe, and Balzac. We pride ourselves upon our frankness in exploring the jungle-land of sexuality, and have some right to do so; yet we follow paths which Richardson and Diderot, Fuseli and Blake, Rossetti and Baudelaire, Webster and Marston trod before us. The phrases differ, the obscene vision is nothing novel, nothing strange. What we experience is, as Emerson would say, an optical illusion, a temporal foreshortening. Perhaps we would estimate talent past and present more temperately if we saw it in full historical perspective.

Historical perspective, however, is precisely what we have no time for. Our age, deeply persuaded of its suicidal tendencies, has become fecund in a Götterdämmerung mythology. Its motto, full of self-pity, is: "So little time," and, faithful to this sentiment, it has no patience with the slow mind of God. Among its characteristic products is the legend of the twenties as a land of Cockaigne. Apparently the twenties arose out of the void. Between the last vestiges of Herman Melville and the first bright saxophone note announcing the coming of Sinclair Lewis, the legend assumes that there was nothing except as Henry Adams, in the character of a New England Wotan, occasioned the building of a sunset bridge over ominous vacuity. Or, to change both the figure and the opera, the American muse in the person of Elsa stood helpless and forlorn until Scott Fitzgerald appeared as Lohengrin that bright April of 1920 when *This Side of Paradise* was published.

The enthusiasm of youth is always charming, and for collegiate youth today the light that never was on sea or land seems to illuminate the nineteen-twenties with its magic glow. The latest Victorian fell, gentlemen preferred blondes, and novelists went out to dine with Cytherea or the tattooed countess. All the sad young men were divinely gay. It was the age of jazz, the age of Mencken, the age of *Main Street,* the age of rebellion. A kind of fawnlike innocence prevailed in an era when *Jurgen* was our utmost in depravity, and Michael Arlen's lady in the green hat knocked at many doors. The fact that serious work was done in the twenties is merely glanced at, for the appeal of the legend lies in its careless gaiety, its paganism, its light mockery, its irresponsibility.

It is, I think, symptomatic that older persons also fall under this fairy spell. Thus Mr. Schulberg's novel, *The Disenchanted,* and Mr. Mizener's biography, *The Far Side of Paradise,* two portraits of Fitzgerald, have had great success.

This Side of Paradise [writes the biographer] connected him in many people's minds with "the Jazz Age," so that he was for them both the historian — "the laureate" — of the post-war generation and its exemplar.

But though Mr. Mizener fights off the legend, he, too, is enchanted, for the next sentence reads:

Perhaps the strongest mark of the early twenties is the widespread conviction — so much stronger than their superficial cynicism — that anyone could do anything; it was a wonderful and inspiriting conviction and encouraged all sorts of people to achievements they might never otherwise have attempted.

I take this to be a tribute to the amateur spirit, which may be well deserved, but when I reflect that the twenties extracted insulin for the first time, began commercial broadcasting, created the talking movies, produced the first long-distance television sets, flew to the North Pole with Admiral Byrd and to Paris with Lindbergh, published *Main Currents in American Thought,*

The Road to Xanadu, Skepticism and Animal Faith,
and *Reconstruction in Philosophy,* painted Marin's
water colors and the earlier work of Charles Sheeler,
domesticated the international style, rescued Brancusi's
"Bird in Flight" from the New York customhouse, and
built both Radburn, New Jersey, and the Museum of
Modern Art, I am not certain that the mere amateur
spirit is a final cause of these expert achievements. Let
me be just to the admirable book of Mr. Mizener, however. From the tragic depths of 1950 the sunlit heights
of 1920 look like eternal youth, eternal spring.

If there is a tendency to envy the period, there is
also a tendency to be condescending. An example, of
considerable interest in Illinois, is Irving Howe's oddly
unsympathetic biography of Sherwood Anderson, published in 1951. Mr. Howe recognizes something called
a Chicago renaissance, reaching its consummate expression, for him, in Margaret Anderson's *Little Review,*
which ended its existence in 1929, in Paris. The renaissance apparently occurred just before the twenties, and
Mr. Howe can find no lasting good in it. Chicago
culture was, he says, "frankly derivative." "A few people
in Chicago," he writes, "were trying hurriedly to create
a culture on the cuff," but it did not come off, the sense
of Europe did not exist, it demanded of its adherents "a
terribly impoverished reading of American literary history," and though Francis Hackett arrived in 1911 to
edit the *Friday Literary Review,* though Floyd Dell
struggled with the circumambient provincialism, Chi-

cago writers "remained smalltownsmen," their "percep-
tion of reality" "insufficient."

I do not quite see how to deal with such compla-
cency. As one who knew Chicago life during this dreary
period of failure, I can only say that at the Chicago Art
Museum I saw for the first time the Armory Show of
1913, including the "Nude Descending a Staircase";
that, expertly played by the Chicago Symphony Orchestra, founded in 1891 by Theodore Thomas and
conducted after 1905 by Frederick Stock, I first heard
Stravinsky's *Le Sacre du Printemps* in this provincial
city; that the only time I ever witnessed Wagner's *Ring*
was in a series of magnificent productions by the Chicago Opera Company in the Chicago Auditorium; that
my first Greek play was Maurice Brown's *The Trojan
Women,* produced in his little theater in the Fine Arts
Building on Michigan Boulevard; that the first book I
ever had published was a translation of Heine's *North
Sea Poems,* brought out by the Open Court Publishing
Company of Chicago, which supported *The Monist,* a
journal of international thought; that almost the first
book review I ever wrote was for *The Dial,* founded in
1880 in Chicago and published there until 1918; that
Marshall Field imported modern furniture from France
before New York or Boston thought of doing so; that
Harriet Monroe's *Poetry,* Ezra Pound being its foreign
correspondent, heralded the new verse after 1912; and
that the Middle West learned about the contemporary
European theater from the *Drama Magazine,* in Chi-

cago from 1911 to 1930. For Mr. Howe the University of Chicago does not exist, but when I remember scholars and writers like Manly, Lovett, Robert Herrick, William A. Nitze, Phillip S. Allen, Tom Peet Cross, Beeson, and Dargan, and scientists like Michaelson, Salisbury, and Carlson — men who seemed to spend as much time in Europe as they did in Illinois — I can only marvel at contemporary standards in biography. Thus it is, however, that legend grows.

II

Let us go back for a look at Scott Fitzgerald. Critics like Malcolm Cowley and Edmund Wilson, anxious that we should comprehend his range and stature, are understandably impatient with the Fitzgerald myth. The grave beauty of *The Great Gatsby* and of that haunting fragment, *The Last Tycoon,* stands in ironic contrast to the fact that "The Crack-Up," Fitzgerald's analogue to Coleridge's "Dejection," was first printed in the pages of *Esquire.* The legend that Fitzgerald was the coryphaeus of the young has, however, its relation to truth. *This Side of Paradise,* a thoroughly juvenile novel, is a primary document, the equivalent of another bad novel by another talented young man, Goethe's *The Sorrows of Werther.* Because, like a well-constructed overture, it contains or foreshadows the motifs of the literary opera that was to come, it deserves analysis, albeit it is my belief that, far from announcing something new, *This*

Side of Paradise was culmination, not revolution — a late expression of a movement linking art, youth, and rebellion, which in one sense began in the 1890's and in another sense, because it is part of the structure of time and modern society, never began at all and therefore begins forever.

This Side of Paradise concerns Amory Blaine, brought up in Minneapolis, sent to Princeton, momentarily touched by World War I, unable to succeed in business and therefore unable to marry, and finally stripped naked by the bankruptcy of the family fortune. The emphasis throughout is personal; that is, blame for the failure of adjustment between personality and society falls upon society, which is thoroughly denounced in a final conversation between Amory Blaine, now, as he thinks, a socialist, and two or three businessmen. This conversation is never menacing, for the reason that the moment Blaine discovers his antagonist is the father of a Princeton classmate killed in action, personalized emotions blanket his social criticism.

The two parts of the novel are entitled, respectively, "The Romantic Egotist" and "The Education of a Personage"; and though it is difficult to say why Amory Blaine is entitled to even this mild compliment, note again the accent on personalism. The book has two epigraphs which further underline the theme. One is from Rupert Brooke: "Well, this side of Paradise . . . There's little comfort in the wise!" The other is mildly misquoted from Oscar Wilde: "Experience is the name so many people give to their mistakes." Rupert Brooke's poem, "Tiare Tahiti," is a satiric attack upon Platonic wisdom by the speaker, a lover of a brown-skinned Gauguin beauty; and Oscar Wilde had argued that art, which never expresses anything but itself, "has an independent life just as Thought has, and develops purely on its own lines," which is tantamount to a claim for the personal autonomy of the artist. The last line of the novel is: "I know myself . . . but that is all," yet we are not to understand that Amory's self-knowledge is Socratic, since for him experience is a simple problem in trial and error, not growth into sagacity.

From his final meditation we learn that in his own judgment selfishness is not only part of him, it is the most living part; that the beauty of great art, the beauty of joy, and the beauty of women are somehow entangled with evil; and that he cannot accept Christianity. Apparently, by "The Education of a Personage" Fitzgerald meant his hero to turn into a lonely Nietzschean, for we read that "in this new loneness of his that had been selected for what greatness he might achieve, beauty must be relative or, itself a harmony, it would make only a discord." Whatever this is supposed to mean, we find the cause of Amory's bitterness both in his renunciation of visual beauty in the person of Rosalind and in the enforced "leaving behind him his chance of being a certain type of artist," which in his case would have been an artist concerned with the art of writing. The

revolt of youth is finally phrased in this meditation as
Amory hears the bells of Princeton:

As an endless dream it went on; the spirit of the past brood-
ing over a new generation, the chosen youth from the
muddled, unchastened world, still fed romantically on the
mistakes and half-forgotten dreams of dead statesmen and
poets. Here was a new generation, shouting the old cries,
learning the old creeds, through a revery of long days and
nights; destined finally to go out into that dirty gray turmoil
to follow love and pride; a new generation dedicated more
than the last to the fear of poverty and the worship of
success; grown up to find all Gods dead, all wars fought, all
faiths in man shaken.

Yet Amory Blaine, by virtue of the very artistic gifts
he is not allowed to exercise, is supposed to have become
a stouter person, "determined to use to the utmost himself and his heritage from the personalities he had
passed." Once more the emphasis is upon personalism.
"Talent doesn't starve any more," Amory informs his
dead friend's father,

Even art gets enough to eat these days. Artists draw your
magazine covers, write your advertisements, hash out rag-
time for your theatres. By the great commercializing of
printing you've found a harmless, polite occupation for every
genius who might have carved his own niche.

But this, precisely, is what Blaine complains of. "I'm
sick of a system," he says, "where the richest man gets
the most beautiful girl if he wants her, where the artist
without income has to sell his talents to a button manu-

facturer." And he plumps for the "natural radical," a type which includes

the congressman you can't bribe, the Presidents who aren't politicians, the writers, speakers, scientists, statesmen who aren't just popular grab-bags for a half dozen women and children.

And in protesting against the worship of the bitch goddess, Success, he protests also against the assumption that human nature never changes and that money is the sole stimulus to endeavor. "Every person over twenty-five years old who makes that statement in cold blood should be deprived of the franchise," hotly declares our hero. But the corruption of business is not the deepest corruption, which is the corruption of the self — "becoming really insincere," says Amory, to whom personality is everything, and theory matters very little.

III

For this emphasis upon self as an ultimate in art I shall shamelessly steal a phrase from Willa Cather. That phrase is *Youth and the Bright Medusa*, title of a book which appeared the same year as *This Side of Paradise*. This title may be taken as a key to, or symbol of, what is central to Amory's notion of himself in *This Side of Paradise* and of what is central in other important books of the twenties — *Main Street*, and *The Waste Land*, and *The Enormous Room*, and *Three Soldiers*, and *Look Homeward, Angel* are examples. All of these books tend to concentrate upon the self as the measure of value. But all these books have a very special self in view. Not the ordinary person, but the self of the artist is in question. From this self no appeal can be made. No matter what scorn is thrown upon other human activities — business, for example, or statesmanship, or the art of war, or the practice of applied science — no doubt whatever is cast upon the validity of the artist and his work. The book may be sceptical about religion, or philosophy, or sex, or patriotism, or education, it is never sceptical about art. Art is autonomous, art is holy, art, even though it bewitch and destroy, does so with the divine right of Apollo, who was empowered both to bless and to ban. And what is true of the artist in the sense of painter, architect, or musician is even more true of the writer, that mover and shaker of things. Let us, like the Greeks, call him the poet and grant him inspiration.

The poet is commonly supposed by these writers to be so by reason of special insight not vouchsafed to the businessman, or the club woman, or the minister, or the lawyer, or the scientist, or the engineer, grosser beings all. Even though in a technological society he depends for his existence upon specialists, specialism does not count, for the poet alone has true knowledge. This true knowledge is the creation of universal Pan, it is a product of Dionysiac insight, it assumes that life in all its manifestations is essentially a dance, it is a kind of magical spell to which readers are expected to yield their judgment, forsaking all others — economists, and historians, and preachers, and generals, and bankers. Because he utters it, the poet's criticism of life possesses finality, and his vision of society, simply because it is his, is ultimate. Finally and inevitably, because poor foolish human life is forever turning away from the shining vision to earn money in our drab and mechanical cities or on our drab and unmechanized farms, the poet, mediating between the vision and reality, between art and society, turns into the radical. Youth rebels because, by the mere fact of being young, it is nearer heaven than are the aging, whose exit from this life it is inclined to pray for. In fact youth rebels even to destruction.

This trilogy of the artist, the poet, and the radical is already present in *This Side of Paradise,* albeit art there tends to take form as fair female flesh and although the muses are translated into Medusa when poor Amory reflects that there is no beauty without some entangling evil. He thus modernizes, as it were, the legend which gives Miss Cather her title. In the myth Medusa was divinely beautiful, but when she violated the sanctity of the temple, she was punished by acquiring the beauty of terror, so much so that whoever looked upon her was turned to stone. Perseus, using his shield as a mirror, so that he looked upon only the reflection of her face, broke the spell. Let us not forget, however, that from the blood of Medusa, Pegasus was born. Only by the death of horror do we come to the horses of inspiration.

The stories which make up *Youth and the Bright*

14

Medusa, seven in number, were written between 1903 and 1920. The best known of them is "Paul's Case," a memorable study of adolescence, illness, obsession with music, the theater, and luxury, and of moral degeneration and eventual suicide. But I shall content myself with some of the others, despite the excellence of this better known narrative. In all these stories the accent is on youth, and the bright Medusa represents the fascination of art, or at least of aesthetic experience, as this works its havoc or its charm. Again and again, tension in these tales arises from the conflict between the desire of the artist to pursue beauty and the necessity of the craftsman, if he is to live, to make some practical adjustment to the workaday world.

An early story is called "The Sculptor's Funeral," dated 1903, a sketch not much beyond the range of a bright literary undergraduate. The theme is the conflict between beauty and reality. A sculptor named Merrick has left the little Kansas village where he was born, gone East, made a success, and died young. Now his disciple, one Steavens, is bringing the body home. Steavens says of his master — and the language is significant — that whatever he touched revealed its holiest secret. The funeral trip is Steavens' first venture into the hinterland, here represented by a raw, ugly, ignorant community in Kansas. He is horrified by the banality of Merrick's home and by the vicious gossip among members and friends of the sculptor's family, none of whom has any comprehension of the life of the free spirit in art.

The climax comes when a drunken lawyer pours his
scorn upon his fellow townsmen in a fashion anticipatory
of *Main Street,* a book not to be published for seven-
teen years. The lawyer and the sculptor had gone to
school together, each had resolved to make something
of himself, but Merrick, by going away, had fulfilled his
ideal, whereas the lawyer had remained and succumbed
to pettiness. "I came back here to practise," he rages,

and I found you didn't in the least want me to be a great
man. . . . I . . . became the damned shyster you wanted
me to be. You pretend to have some sort of respect for me,
and yet you'll stand up and throw mud at Harvey Merrick,
whose soul you couldn't dirty and whose hands you couldn't
tie. . . . Now that we've fought and lied and sweated and
stolen and hated as only the disappointed strugglers in a
bitter, dead little Western town know how to do, what have
we got to show for it?

The last glimpse vouchsafed us of the dead sculptor's
face shows him "still guarding something precious."

Obviously this is 'prentice work, which offers very
little new. The drabness and cruelty of American village
life had furnished a theme for Ed Howe's *Story of a
Country Town* in 1883, and the escape of aesthetic
youth into the city had been in part the theme of Gar-
land's *Rose of Dutcher's Coolly* in 1895. The lawyer's
speech is heavy-handed. But it is for that very reason
revealing. The story is at once a passionate defense of
youth and art, which keep from others "something
precious," and a passionate denunciation of American

domesticity and of small-town democracy. Merrick's death is immaterial; what matters is Merrick's life, dedicated to self-fulfillment. That life represented the revolt of youth in the service of art against customary culture. Merrick had never, as Scott Fitzgerald would say, become "really insincere."

This theme is more subtly treated in the latest story of the volume, one entitled, "Coming, Aphrodite!" This is mature, even though the central episode sounds a bit ridiculous in the telling; and in order to get the ridicule out of the way, let me say that it concerns a young man staring every afternoon through a knothole in his bedroom closet at a naked young woman doing exercises in the next apartment. The fact that Miss Cather raises this episode from the vulgarity of voyeurism to beauty shows how she had developed between 1903 and 1920.

The tale concerns one Hedger, a painter, living in a ramshackle apartment house in Washington Square. Into the adjoining apartment moves Edna, or Eden, Bower, already on the road to becoming a successful opera singer. She has come to New York to stay until a wealthy Chicagoan and his sister are ready to take her to Europe. Eden is vigorous, attractive, healthy, curious; and after some preliminary stages of irritation, Hedger falls in love with her, for, as he watches her naked body, it seems to his painter's eye, utterly beautiful. Their acquaintance ripens; and when she learns of his peeping, she is not offended. They go to Coney Island, where

Eden once more irritates Hedger by substituting, on
impulse, for a trapeze artist making a balloon ascension.
Since part of the trick is that an evening gown shall fall
from the shoulders of the trapeze artist, revealing a lady
in tights, Hedger is again annoyed, but the annoyance
leads into the love affair, which is happy and healthy
and pagan.

However, Eden Bower is a musical performer on the
make rather than a creator; and since she knows it takes
money and backing to succeed in the concert world,
she assumes the same conditions exist in the world of
painting. When, therefore, she has wheedled a fashion-
able portrait painter into taking some notice of her
lover, she is furious to discover that Hedger will have
nothing to do either with the society racket or with
commercialism. He rests content in his youthful integrity. They quarrel. He leaves, and when, remorseful, he
returns, he discovers that Eden's wealthy patrons have
carried her off to Europe, leaving him a memory, a
dressing gown, and a letter.

What Miss Cather writes about Eden's childhood is
pertinent to our theme:

People like Eden Bower are inexplicable. Her father sold
farming machinery in Huntington, Illinois, and she had
grown up with no acquaintance or experiences outside of that
prairie town. Yet from her earliest childhood she had not
one conviction or opinion in common with the people about
her — the only people she knew. Before she was out of short
dresses she had made up her mind that she was going to be
an actress, that she would live far away in great cities, that

she would be much admired by men and would have everything she wanted. When she was thirteen, and was already singing and reciting for church entertainments, she read in some illustrated magazine a long article about the late Tsar of Russia, then just come to the throne or about to come to it. After that, lying in the hammock on the front porch on summer evenings, or sitting through a long sermon in the family pew, she amused herself by trying to make up her mind whether she would or would not be the Tsar's mistress when she played in his capital. Now Edna had met this fascinating word only in the novels of Ouida — her hardworked little mother kept a long row of them in the upstairs storeroom, behind the linen closet. In Huntington women who bore that relation to men were called by a very different name, and their lot was not an enviable one; of all the shabby and poor, they were the shabbiest. But then, Edna had never lived in Huntington, not even before she began to find books like "Sapho" and "Mademoiselle de Maupin" secretly sold in paper covers through Illinois. It was as if she had come into Huntington, into the Bower family, on one of the trains that puffed over the marshes behind their back fence all day long, and was waiting for another train to take her out.

You will note that in this passage the birth of an artist is inexplicable — that is, it is placed outside the ordinary chain of cause and effect.

In "The Sculptor's Funeral" Miss Cather's purpose was principally to indict. The village heretic there is merely a mouthpiece for the author, the dead sculptor is a stereotype, and his friend Steavens, through whose eyes the conflict between art and reality is revealed, is but the shadow of a shade. In "Coming, Aphrodite!"

however, two human beings are fully studied in their strength and their weakness. Miss Cather does not manage the story, nor does she insist upon a moral. If, from Hedger's point of view, Eden betrays the high responsibility of the artist who must never compromise his vision, to Eden, Hedger is an obstinate, impatient, impractical young man with small sense of humor and no willingness to have fun. She cannot understand why he does not appreciate her lowering her own pride in order to wheedle a successful painter into looking at Hedger's work.

But though Miss Cather is apparently impartial, when we analyze what she tells us of Eden's childhood, we discover a deft indictment of American domesticity. Family life, village life are again represented as hostile to the artist. We read that Eden is inexplicable as a product of Huntington — as if the artist were somehow a miraculous creation. We learn that she and the community had not a single conviction or opinion in common. Her dream was, as soon as she could, to flee to the metropolis, to develop her personality, to be admired, and to escape vulgarity, especially the crass polarity of female types in the village — whores or wives. Her father sells farm machinery, her mother is hardworked and hides naughty novels behind the linen closet. We learn nothing else about Eden's girlhood except that somehow or other she must have submitted to the discipline of music lessons, that she was bored on Sundays, and that, on long summer evenings, dreaming in the hammock, she thought a great deal was going to happen to her. The story concerns one of the earlier stages in her making things happen; and if Eden's adolescent notions of luxury are naive, we must remember that her information was limited.

Yet, for all her seeming impartiality, Miss Cather makes one deadly comment when she writes that Eden "did not guess her neighbor [Hedger] would have more tempestuous adventures sitting in his dark studio than she would find in all the capitals of Europe, or in all the latitude of conduct that she was prepared to permit herself." If Miss Cather recognizes the validity of the revolt of youth in the name of art, she also insists upon an essential difference between the ethos of the artist — in this case, Hedger — and the ethos of the mere practitioner, or follower — in this case, Eden Bower. If life is to be lived experimentally, it makes a great deal of difference by whom the experiment is conducted. Unlike Fitzgerald, Miss Cather, in addition to dramatizing the revolt of youth in the name of art, evaluated as well the rebel personality.

IV

Other stories in the collection concern the central conflict between the arts and the economic order; as, for example, the right of relatives to exploit a singer. But for richer treatment of the ambivalent lure of art one turns to her novels. The earliest, *Alexander's Bridge,* appeared in 1912. Bartley Alexander, a successful builder of bridges, comfortably married to a Boston wife and apparently happy, rediscovers on a solitary business trip to London that Hilda Burgoyne, the lost love of his youth, has become a mature and fascinating actress. Despite every effort of his moral will, he succumbs to the timeless promise, the immortal memory of youth and art. The climax comes with the simultaneous collapse of a bridge, built too near the safety margin, and of Alexander, who dies in the river, a victim of a similar error in the human equation. Hilda lives, on the whole enriched as an artist by suffering because she represents the autonomy of art. The story is in ten chapters and an epilogue; precisely at the end of the fifth chapter we find this tribute to universal Pan:

But Alexander was not thinking about his work. After the fourth night out [on the steamer taking him back to London], when his will suddenly softened under his hands, he had been continually hammering away at himself. More and more often, when he first awakened in the morning or when he stepped into a warm place after being chilled on the deck, he felt a sudden painful delight at being nearer another shore. Sometimes, when he was most despondent, when he thought himself worn out with this struggle, in a flash he was free of it and leaped into an overwhelming consciousness of himself. On the instant he felt that marvellous return of the impetuousness, the intense excitement, the increasing expectancy of youth.

In view of the pagan mysticism of this passage one almost expects Bartley to have sight of Proteus rising from the sea. He is the victim of the Dionysiac fascination, the Bacchic appeal, the illusion of youth, which create in him a new and overwhelming feeling of self, sensed in a series of mystical insights superior to his normal self and eventually controlling it.

Alexander's Bridge dwells upon the destructive powers of the bright Medusa, but in *The Song of the Lark* three years later Miss Cather reversed the legend and wrote a profound and subtle study of the growth into selfhood of a great artist, tracing the life of Thea Kronborg from her childhood in Moonstone, Colorado, to golden triumph as a Wagnerian singer at the Metropolitan. The title comes from Millet's painting, "The Song of the Lark," in the Chicago Art Institute, not from Thea's voice, and the picture is chiefly significant in the novel as a symbol of wordless communication between the peasant girl and the unseen singer in the sky. In a preface dated 1932 Miss Cather was unnecessarily apologetic about what she calls the descending curve of the story — that is, she argued that the life of the successful artist is less interesting than the life of a talented young girl making her way. Perhaps so. What I think more important is that she also points out she had reversed *The Portrait of Dorian Gray* by Oscar Wilde. As Thea is more and more released into artistic fulfillment, her life as artist becomes more self-absorbed and her life as person grows less interesting. Only as artist is she happy, free, and real.

Certain basic elements in the story require analysis. One notes the assumption that there exists a secret community of persons capable of discovering and accepting instinctive values — a mystery cult of art, a fraternity of the initiate. Let us borrow a phrase from Schumann's famous piano piece and call this the *Davidsbündler* — the League of David against the Philistines. Training does not bring one initiation, only temperament can do that. Thus Thea's vocal teacher does not "belong," whereas the Mexicans in Moonstone enjoy membership — visiting them, she found "there was no constraint of any kind . . . but a kind of natural harmony." As Wunsch, Thea's first teacher, tells her: "Some things cannot be taught. If you do not know in the beginning, you do not know in the end." Though Thea cannot communicate her deepest thoughts to the devoted pianist, Harsanyi, he understands her because he too was born a member of the *Davidsbündler*. He realizes that "one must take where and when one can the mysterious mental irritant that rouses one's imagination . . . it is not to be had by order." The *Davidsbündler* is a race apart — Thea's birthright in it is symbolized by her acquiring a room of her own in the crowded household — and forms a natural league against the Philistines. As Thea tells her devoted admirer, Doctor Archie:

If you love the good thing you must hate the cheap thing just as hard. I tell you there is such a thing as creative hate! A contempt that drives you through fire, makes you risk everything and lose everything, makes you a long sight better than you ever knew you could be.

The section of the book in which Thea breaks with her family is entitled "Stupid Faces," and it is against the stupid faces of the world that the artist must rebel.

A second component is passion — not necessarily the passion of love, but will, strength, an unquenchable vitality that creates the self. That Thea possesses passion in this sense comes to her in successive revelations. When Wunsch first implies that she is destined for something better than Moonstone, she is shaken by a passion of excitement, she feels a kind of "warm sureness." She develops the will to effort, she overcomes difficulties without verbal comprehension of them, she lifts, as it were, weights greater than herself. After her first experience of symphonic music, a great rush of power floods her being, making her hands cold with excitement, and it seems to her a hostile world would like to rob her of this vitality, but, she meditates, "As long as she lived that ecstasy was going to be hers. She would live for it, work for it, die for it." At the end of the novel Harsanyi's comment is: "Her secret? It is every artist's secret . . . passion. That is all. It is an open secret, and perfectly safe. Like heroism, it is inimitable in cheap materials." And at the moment of her triumph as Sieglinde: "Not for nothing had she kept it so severely, kept it filled with such energy and fire. All that deep-rooted vitality flowered in her voice, in her very finger-tips. She felt like a tree bursting into bloom."

But the vitality is expendable, the tree must have its roots and sap. Nourishment of the artist's self depends upon an intermingling of the senses and the soul. This neither conventional ethics nor Philistine psychology can ever comprehend. The sensuous renewal comes to Thea at intervals, but never more importantly than in Part IV, entitled "The Ancient People," when she goes out to an Arizona canyon near an abandoned cliff-dwelling. Note how, in the introductory paragraph, Miss Cather sets the stage for this part of the story, insisting upon selfhood, incommunicability, and the healing power of an ancient, chthonic way of life:

The San Francisco Mountain lies in northern Arizona, above Flagstaff, and its blue slopes and snowy summit entice the eye for a hundred miles across the desert. About its base lie the pine forests of the Navajos, where the great red-trunked trees live out their peaceful centuries in that sparkling air. The piñons and scrub begin only where the forest ends, where the country breaks into open, stony clearings, and the surface of the earth cracks into deep canyons. The great pines stand at a considerable distance from each other. Each tree grows alone, murmurs alone, thinks alone. They do not obtrude upon each other. The Navajos are not much in the habit of giving or of asking help. Their language is not a communicative one, and they never attempt an interchange of personality in speech. Over their forests there is the same inexorable reserve. Each tree has its exalted power to bear.

Into this silence Thea Kronborg comes from her struggle in the city, and there she learns the last secret of selfhood and of art. She had got back to the earliest sources of gladness that she could remember — the sun, the brilliant sand, the sky, the night. Slowly music comes to her as sensuous form rather than something to be struggled with. Her power of thought ceases to be intellection or communication, it is converted "into a power of sustained sensation. She could become a mere receptacle for heat . . . or . . . color . . . or a continuous repetition of sound." In this fallow mood her love affair with Fred Ottenburg, who is married, though Thea does not know it at the time, is merely part of the world of sense and soul, so that what might have broken a Philistine is for her an increment. The last secret is this:

The stream and the broken pottery: what was any art but an effort to make a sheath, a mould in which to imprison for a moment the shining, elusive element which is life itself — life hurrying past us and running away, too strong to stop, too sweet to lose? The Indian women had held it in their jars. In the sculpture she had seen in the Art Institute, it had been caught in a flash of arrested motion. In singing one made a vessel of one's throat and nostrils and held it on one's breath, caught the stream in a scale of natural intervals.

Much earlier in the story Thea had had a foreshadowing of this experience, when, as she lay in her hard-won little room, "life rushed in upon her through that window — or so it seemed," but, comments Miss Cather,

In reality, life rushes from within, not from without. There is no work of art so big or so beautiful that it was not once all contained in some youthful body like this one which lay on the floor in the moonlight, pulsing with ardor and anticipation.

So, in her fulfilling time, in the ancient canyons of Arizona, youth and art to Thea Kronborg become time-less and one thing, for the paradoxical reason that youth is translated out of time into form and energy.

Finally, the completed act of art is a completed act of truth. Neither Thea nor her creator can tell us the way by which she comes to truth, all they can tell us is that she finds it and unshakably knows she has found it. The story of her musical education — that is, of the development of the artist into maturity — is a chronicle of the inadequacy of words to communicate meaning. Wunsch finds in her "something unconscious and un-awakened," but he cannot touch her with speech. She is unable to talk to Harsanyi, largely because of this doctrine of the secret — something to be guarded against the Philistines. Miss Cather writes of her:

Hitherto she had felt but one obligation toward [her genius] — secrecy; to protect it even from herself. She had always believed that by doing all that was required of her by her family, her teachers, her pupils, she kept that part of herself from being caught up in the meshes of common things. . . . It was as if she had an appointment to meet the rest of herself sometime, somewhere.

Once, singing for Harsanyi, she sings wrong, he tries to correct her, he gets nowhere, and then suddenly light dawns, and Harsanyi meditates:

He had often noticed that she could not think a thing out in passages. Until she saw it as a whole, she wandered like a blind man surrounded by torments. After she once had her "revelation," after she had got the idea that to her — not always to him — explained everything, then she went forward rapidly. But she was not always easy to help.

Yet at the very end of the novel Miss Cather's comment is:

Artistic growth is, more than anything else, a refining of the sense of truthfulness. The stupid believe that to be truthful is easy; only the artist, the great artist knows how difficult it is.

Whether this organicism, this non-rational approach (one scarcely knows whether to call it supra-rational or sub-rational) be sound or socially right — it has embarrassing relations to the doctrine of thinking with one's blood — there is an eternal contradiction between artistic truth arrived at by instinct and revelation, and the truth of a world in which analysis and computation — the slide rule, the butcher's scale, the bank balance, the chemist's analysis — are paramount.

If Miss Cather's subtle study of the development of youth into art antedates and diminishes *This Side of Paradise,* it is a commonplace of literary history that *The Song of the Lark* in turn had its predecessors — Robert Herrick's *The Common Lot* (1904), a study of an architect; Theodore Dreiser's *Sister Carrie* (1900), in which a huge and vital tide carries Carrie Meeber to success on the stage; or the three novels of Arlo Bates, *The Pagans* (1884), *The Philistines* (1889), and *The Puritans* (1898), which, dated in many respects, yet have the root of the matter in them. Of about 125 fictional titles by Henry James something over a fifth have to do with the development of the artist — painter, actress, writer — with the nature of artistic truth, and with the irrelevance of secular measurements of the divine fire. Typical is *The Tragic Muse* (1890), in which, by contrary motion, Nicholas Dormer gives up matrimony and politics for painting, and Miriam Rooth gives up domesticity for acting and matrimony. Two passages illustrate James's adumbration of the theme. Of political speaking Dormer roundly says, "It has nothing to do with the truth, or the search for it; nothing to do with intelligence, or candor, or honor." In contrast, the fascination of art, embodied in Miriam Rooth, is thus set forth:

But the great thing, to his mind and, these first days, the irresistible seduction of the theatre, was that she was a rare incarnation of beauty. Beauty was the principle of everything she did and of the way, unerringly, she did it — the exquisite harmony of line and motion and attitude and tone, what was most general and most characteristic in her performance. Accidents and instincts played together to this end and constituted something which was independent of her talent or her merit, in a given case, and which in its influence . . . was far superior to any merit and to any talent. It was a supreme infallible felicity, a source of importance, a stamp of absolute value. To see it in operation, to sit within its radius and feel it shift and revolve and change and never fail, was a corrective to the depression, the humiliation, the bewilderment of life.

This is persuasively, this is beautifully said, but if, like jesting Pilate, we ask what is truth and unlike him, stay for answer, no clear explanation is forthcoming. The assertion that superior truth is expressed by the artist raises the same difficulties that appear when a great religious leader asserts that he expresses superior truth. In *Varieties of Religious Experience* William James examined the various modes by which the religious person comes to the belief that he has or has had a special vision of truth, but so far as I am aware, no one has made a similar study of varieties of religious experience, so to say, expressed as art. Our studies of aesthetic principles are, perhaps rightly, metaphysical and formal; but when the artist abandons any formal system of values and of truth — say, for example, Platonic philosophy or Christian belief—he faces very great difficulties. And these difficulties are not the sort arising out of the old Art-for-Art's-sake movement, inasmuch as the modern artist does not, like these earlier men, give up the ethical problem as irrelevant, but on the contrary assumes that the ethical problem is solved in the work of art itself. If one burns with a hard, gemlike flame, if one lives so that he can say to this or that passing moment, "Tarry awhile, thou art so fair," individual experience is, indeed, the center of the statement, but no assumption is made about human dignity, whereas the tacit assumption of Miss Cather and, for that matter, of Scott Fitzgerald, is that human dignity is enhanced in being the creator of a work of art — an assumption which becomes more and more perilous, the more one meditates upon it and upon the biographies of artists, particularly those of artists in modern times. It is a theory which requires a greater degree of support than solipsism can offer, and yet no very clear sustaining hypothesis seems to be at hand. It is sometimes said the artist may be sustained by something called myth, and it is sometimes said he is sustained by something called culture or society.

Let us glance at some attempts to remake myth in the name of art, and at certain aspects of the artist's relation to culture, particularly to republican culture. I prefer this term as having certain theoretic values not found in a phrase like "the democratic way of life," an awkward concept to keep clear of mere propaganda. But first, for art and myth.

2

THE *Poet*

In the phrase "Youth and the Bright Medusa" we agree to embody the enigmatic lure which the life of art often holds for youth, and which it held most evidently and most disastrously for youth in the nineteen-twenties. The pathetic career of Scott Fitzgerald, partially foreshadowed in *This Side of Paradise,* dramatizes a legend, and at the end of that decade — that is, in 1929 — *Look Homeward, Angel* announced another heaven-storming genius that burned itself out too quickly in the name of art. In a general sense, since the death of Thomas Wolfe, the youth movement has virtually disappeared, but it has not utterly vanished. Contemporary writing has produced other sacrifices to the bright Medusa which it might be embarrassing to discuss. And our problem is a two-fold one: to ascertain whether this youth movement is what legend makes it out to be — a product of postwar disillusion in the twenties, or whether its sources and significance are not deeper and more important than, let us say, the light of Miss Millay's candle which, burning at both ends, shed on friend and foe its lovely and ephemeral light. This inquiry in turn leads into the second question: what support can be given the implied doctrine of a superior truth in art, supposed to justify the sacrifice of youth?

I have assumed that special light is shed on the nature of an artist's development (especially on the nature of development of art into truth) in the fiction of Willa Cather; and if I seem to slight the claims of Henry James in this regard, it is not because his fiction fails to interest itself in art and in artists. True, he says little about music, but his narratives do concern the sculptor, the painter, the actress, and the writer. But there is a radical difference between the approach of Henry James to this problem and the approach of Willa Cather. For James the problem is one of culture; for Miss Cather it is a problem of energy. The one pays homage to Apollo, the other to Dionysius, and though both agree that the artist is possessed of a secret and superior truth, for James the problem is Platonic, whereas Miss Cather narrates the unfolding of her singer in terms of Orphic initiation. Culture, it is James's hope, will eventually lead into that study of perfection which is art; but in Miss Cather's world the initiates already recognize each other by signs too subtle for the multitude. Art for the one is wisdom; for the other it is radiance.

I have remarked that difficulties arise from the hypothesis that the artist, by reason of nature and nurture, has a special power of expressing immediate truth. The truth of science, it is commonplace, is subject to verification. Anybody may repeat the experiment and arrive at the inference, provided he have proper training and equipment. Even though scientific hypothesis depends in marked degree upon the creative imagination, it does not remain within the realm of imagination, it is not truth *eo ipso* because of its mode of expression; and though in a loose sense one can speak of a scientific "type," the personality of the scientist is not a principal reason for accepting what he utters as being therefore true. In all these particulars, however, the artist makes an opposite claim. This claim is pushed to an extreme limit in modern times. The work of a Joyce or a Faulkner, an Archipenko or an Alexander Calder, a Burchfield or a Mark Tobey, a Stravinsky or a Walter Piston cannot be verified by common sense. No other person can do what each of them uniquely does. Each translation of experience into form by the modern artist is, and is supposed to be, private and therefore lonely in greater or less degree.

I open Oliver Larkin's *Art and Life in America* and read concerning the work of a contemporary sculptor:

The *Young Girl* of David Hare was the work of a man who refused to be objective about a particular young girl, and its fragmentary references to lips, teeth, breasts, and thighs were arbitrarily assembled to suggest a movement which, continued in the mind of the observer, would create a form unlike any which had yet existed.

The accompanying picture shows an object something like a pair of sugar tongs surrounding a keyhole and surmounted by a button hook; halfway up the button hook are mounted two smaller objects suggesting door-stops extended toward the observer, and the interior curve of the button-hook handle is ornamented by half a dozen projections supposed to hint at teeth. I am deliberately unkind in describing Mr. Hare's statue in order to call attention to the extraordinary degree to which subjectivity has been pushed by the modern artist. The spectator is left only with the privilege of rejection.

Undoubtedly a minority of beholders find in the object, because of its title, its flow of line, its suggestion of certain Freudian symbols, a satisfactory reference to the quintessence of young girlhood, but I suspect the majority are merely bewildered, especially if, when they inquire of the modern sculptor what his statue means, they are answered: "Why, the statue speaks for itself. If you don't see what it means, it means nothing to you. But it means a great deal to me." In sum, the meaning of a work of art is the work of art. As Aaron Copland put it recently, the composer of a piece of music says to the auditor: did my piece hold your attention? Yes. Then that is the meaning of the piece. Or, to translate the idea into terms of yet another art,

> A poem should not mean
> But be.

As I have no special competence in aesthetics, meta-physics, or psychology, I shall not inquire further into the validity of this form of the doctrine of the autonomy of art. Great claims are made on its behalf by theorists, who tend to assume that those who demand some degree of representation in art — that is, some correlation between the mode of expression and the subject of the work — are Philistines and therefore the enemies of the *Davidsbündler*. What is more relevant is to note the increased demand upon the energy of the artist in modern times.

II

During the long centuries when art was primarily religious ritual — rock-painting, image-making, dancing, the drama, or legend-telling; and while the artist was still priest or prophet rather than aesthete, this burden was not felt. To know the right formula for the fertility dance, to be able to costume the dancers, to propitiate the gods of thunder or of drought by appropriate ceremony, to utter prayers which would compel the spirits of the departed to assist the tribe, to make proper sand-drawings against sickness, to recite upon ceremonial occasions the ancient wisdom — when such was the primary function of art, the artist-priest was socially and philosophically effective. At a simple cultural level an anecdote preserved in the *Britannica* illustrates the point. A sorcerer named Tata Ko told the British governor of Papua, New Guinea:

If a man falls sick, his family come to me and ask me to make him well. If I don't do something for him, they say,

"Tata Ko, the sorcerer, desires to kill our brother," and they are angry and will perhaps try to kill me. If I do give them something, they insist on paying me well for it; should I refuse to take their presents, they would not understand it and they would think I am trying to kill their friend.

In Papua, it is clear, the artist as magician-priest fulfilled a religious function which involves no question of genius, originality, or personal style.

If we pass to a higher cultural level — that, for example, represented by the Greek anthology — we see how the works of artists and artificers — fish-nets, cups, statues, sandals, flutes, the prows of ships, the shields of warriors — exist to praise the gods. A poem by Paulus the Silentiary concerning an aging calligrapher named Callimenes is pertinent:

Here Callimenes, his eye and hand enfeebled by age, dedicates to the laughter-loving Muses the never-moistened lead which draws that undeviating line on which is based the regularity of the script, the ruler which guides the course of this revolving lead, the porous stone like a sponge, the receptacle of the permanent ink, the pens themselves, too, their tips dyed black, the sponge, flower of the sea, forming the meadows of the liquid deep, and the knife, brazen artificer of slender pens.

A modern novelist is unlikely to hang his typewriter in a church as a votive offering, and the fact that even museums are chary of accepting such relics as the pens with which poets wrote or the chair in which some favorite author sat is evidence of our break with the religious sanction of art.

On a still higher level one notes how the great Greek poets were content with a profound lack of originality. Greek drama was ritual. The occasion, the subject, the form of this ritual were all prescribed, so that dramatists, unlike modern musicians, did not have incessantly to invent new themes, new styles, new treatments for fear of being charged with imitation. On the contrary the Greek writer of tragedy displayed his genius in accepting what was prescribed and then, by adapting ritual to life, satisfying the desire of his audience for meanings that were simultaneously sanctioned by custom and applicable to the day.

When we pass into Christian art — Saracenic would do as well — we note the continuance of the same kind of assumption. What seems to us rigid in Byzantine mosaics, for example, is not so much rigidity as the result of the truth that form, subject, and occasion were part of ritual. In the Middle Ages the prescribed story of Christianity satisfied everybody from the humblest carpenter helping to produce the Noah's-ark play to the lofty genius of Dante; and the simple assumption that the substance of art is prescribed passed over into secular literature. Medieval romances are invariably old, or, if they are not, they pretend to be. Chaucer invents nothing, he retells everything on authority, just as the medieval altar piece is never original, the book of the hours a miracle of inherited patterns, the cathedral a building in which tradition governs all. So it is with early Italian painting — its masters did not have to invent St. Sebastian, or the Virgin, or the Crucifixion, but were free to concentrate upon treatment and delight. When, by and by, Western culture assimilated a new version of the classical past to the Christian legend, the subjects of painting and sculpture, poetry and music, the drama and the dance were still, in some sense, prescribed. Even Shakespeare does not "invent" a play as Dickens or Faulkner invents a novel. And though Shakespeare once lamented the public means which public manners breed, it is more characteristic of Renaissance culture to assume that genius is somehow Platonic, or at any rate Apollonian, rather than Byronic and anarchical. Eventually the doctrine that genius is unique replaced the doctrine that genius is normative.

During the last three centuries, partly as result and partly as cause, the prophetic or ritualistic function of the artist has disappeared with the disappearance of unified faith. The result has been to subject him to unusual economic hardship. His goods are merely luxury goods, sold in a competitive market and vying with baseball, perfume, and automobiles. The disastrous result in American painting and sculpture is evident from Elizabeth McCausland's finding that in 1947, after twenty years spent in the practice of art, the average American painter earned only $1,154 a year from the sale of his product. The situation has not grown better since. In the field of music the late Serge Koussevitzky in 1946 could find no hope except from government. He said: "We, artists, are the living pulses of art; the state is the grounds upon which art finds stability and security. It is imperative for the state to realize and acknowledge the signal need of our time." Whether a department of music in the Cabinet at the present time would improve that art is anybody's guess.

As for literature, from Howells' penetrating essay in the nineties, "The Man of Letters as a Man of Business" through James T. Farrell's grim "The Fate of Writing in America" (1945) to C. Hartley Grattan's article in *Harper's* last November, the complaint deepens in gravity. The writer cannot write and live. Says Mr. Grattan: "What I am leading up to is the point that writers cannot write good books at any level of excellence if they are badgered to death by economic worries. Mostly today they are so badgered, and the situation seems constantly to be worsening."

Equally disastrous has been the divorce of the substance of art from faith and from myth. Whether he intended it so or not, the decree of Pope Pius X inculcating the restoration of the style of Palestrina for liturgical music in the Roman Catholic Church drove a wedge between the largest Christian body in the world and the contemporary composer. The days of Christian music *per se* are now virtually over. As for painting, sculpture, and architecture, Father M. A. Vouturier, writing in the *Magazine of Art* last November, noted as a unique fact that three small churches in France had been decorated by moderns, including Matisse, Chagall, Braque, and Rouault, who has had to wait until he was eighty before any canvas of his was admitted into a church. Father Vouturier remarks: "One is forced to admit that Christian art is dead. . . . For more than a century, imagination — the true innovator of all new forms — has remained completely outside of, and alien to, the Church." He is not even sure the artists named are Christians, but he comforts himself by saying that the true sources of art do not lie in conscious choice and rational thought, but in the subliminal realm of consciousness, that secret and persistent realm of childhood where deep, mysterious Christian sources never deteriorate.

Whatever the validity of this theological version of the psychiatric problem, no modern — not even Mr. T. S. Eliot — is a Christian writer in the sense that Boethius and Dante, St. Theresa and St. John of the Cross, John Woolman and John Bunyan were, in their respective fashions, among the *animae naturaliter christianiae*. Until Mr. Eliot's proclamation that he was conservative, Christian, and royalist — the last adjective turned him into a subject of King George — I suppose Henry Wadsworth Longfellow, when after thirty years of thought, his dramatic trilogy, *Christus: A Mystery,* appeared, was the last American writer of stature to make Christianity the central theme of a large-scale poetical work. The Greek gods, moreover, have never been domesticated in America, where we have likewise failed to domesticate either the gods of the Nibelungs or the myths of the North American Indians, so that, though we have developed folklore figures like Paul Bunyan and Uncle Tom, myth with us, except in so far as Freudianism involves anthropological concepts, is artificial and "literary."

The modern American writer, like the modern artist, belongs to no traditional faith and has no traditional body of material, religious, mytho-poetic, ritualistic, or racial, to refashion. The remote relation of a contemporary musical composition to the original dance-forms out of which the symphony was born, measures the depth of our descent into a gulf where the artist and the author stand naked and alone, trying to hold up the sky with their fingers. The extreme isolation of the moderns is described in a paragraph from Mr. John W. Aldridge's *After the Last Generation,* an inquiry into the work of a dozen younger writers. Mr. Aldridge says:

Nearly all the old primary assumptions which men once took for granted — the idea of one god and of a very few fixed doctrines suitable to his worship, of a fixed code of sexual and social morality, of a fixed dichotomous universe divided between the two irreconcilable forces of Good and Evil — have been slowly but relentlessly eroded away by the advancement of natural sciences, philosophy, and, particularly, psychology; or, to put it more precisely, they have been dissected and atomized until they have lost the authority of a single, integrated body of belief and been scattered into countless fragments of comfortless superstition, vague longing, and abortive guilt.

Upon this, and similar passages, Mr. Grattan's comment is that writers in all countries have "lost the capacity of assuming that, at bottom, they know what the life of man is all about."

III

I suggested that the importance of Fitzgerald and of *This Side of Paradise* lies not so much in any putative greatness in the man or perfection in the book as in the typicality of both. At the end of this adolescent novel Amory Blaine also stands naked and alone. Art, love, war, business, and religion have all failed him. "I know myself," he says, which is patently not true. His pose is artificial and jejune. Yet the mixed bravado and desperation of "The Crack-Up" by this same writer reveals the mature Fitzgerald's sense of motion in a vacuum, energy spent on empty space. So, too, Amory Blaine's search preludes a wilder search that began in 1929 when Tom Wolfe published the first of his four vast novels, all about himself. He assured his readers that he and they and we are all lost, and he dedicated his energies to searching — for what?

The deepest search in life, it seemed to me, the thing that in one way or another was central to all living was man's search for a father, not merely the father of his flesh, not merely the lost father of his youth, but the image of a strength and wisdom external to his need and superior to his hunger, to which the belief and power of his own life could be united.

44

For Wolfe the smile of the bright Medusa meant self-destruction. "In order to belong to a rare and higher breed," he wrote, "one must first develop the true power and talent of selfless immolation," and he thought of himself as the mystical bearer of the Word in the sense of a secular Logos, a "Word" which should include "the interests and designs of his fellow men and of all humanity."

But to stretch yourself to embrace "all humanity" is to destroy yourself, as Wolfe destroyed himself in the desire to go everywhere and to experience everything. In the absence of any myth which might permit a process of identification he strove to create one — the father image, the "Word," the mother, the fecund earth, but all in vain. So, too, Hart Crane, stretching both himself and the image of Brooklyn Bridge until both collapsed, tried simultaneously to create mythology and to wreak himself upon all experience. So Ernest Hemingway, finding as it were the repetition on a Tibetan prayer wheel, of Nada, Nada, Nada unsatisfactory, has struggled to turn death into ritual, to find in the formalities of the bullfight and in an ancient grace in dying, evidence of a masculine deity, nameless and Janus-faced, who shall be at once the life-giver and the destroyer. Or, finally, one may note how a poet like Robinson Jeffers has striven to turn stallions, eagles, rocks, and primal lusts into a private mythology of his own devising.

At this point the old-fashioned neo-humanist is

likely to say something owlish about the deficiencies of
the romantic conception of genius. But if we content
ourselves with the smaller arc of our own literary development, we can push the poet's quest for modern
myth back through Henry Adams' dynamo and virgin,
Whitman's doctrine of comrades, Captain Ahab, the

> sweet clay from the breast
> Of the unexhausted West

out of which Lowell derived Abraham Lincoln, Longfellow's Hiawatha and Cooper's Leatherstocking to
those unreadable epics in which the Connecticut Wits
spoke of Columbus and Columbia and Canaan. This,
however, would be less revealing than to pause in the
Harvard Yard during the middle nineties and examine
a poetic renaissance which has been either forgotten or
underestimated. In language that seems to us old-
fashioned but that is nonetheless passionate and sincere,
a group of younger writers — Trumbull Stickney, George
Cabot Lodge, George Santayana, and William Vaughn
Moody — were struggling with the same problem as
were the men of the twenties and the thirties. For them,
as for the last generation, all the primary assumptions
had collapsed. Heirs of a Christian tradition without
Christian belief and of a cultural tradition without any
central mytho-poetic core, they lived in a universe
relentlessly eroded by the advancement of natural
sciences. Unlike the moderns, burdened in Mr. Aldridge's language with "comfortless superstition, vague

longing, and abortive guilt," these writers affirmed a faith in humanity opposite to the negativism of later days. I turn to their treatment of the modern problems of the poet and of poetic truth.

IV

The movement in question began with the publication of Santayana's *Sonnets and Other Verses* in 1894 (unless one wants to count poems in magazines prior to this date) and may be said to end with Moody's *Poems and Poetic Dramas* in 1912. The evidence includes about sixteen books of poetry, much of it in dramatic form, together with an indefinite amount of periodical material. If we were to study exhaustively the intellectual setting of the group, we should have to analyze such books as Josiah Royce's *The Conception of God* (1897), William James's *The Varieties of Religious Experience* (1902), Santayana's *The Life of Reason* (1905-06), and William Sturgis Bigelow's *Buddhism and Immortality* (1908). A wider circle would include writers like Bernhard Berenson, Robert Herrick, Robert Morss Lovett, H. T. Parker, Edwin Arlington Robinson, Norman Hapgood, and George Pierce Baker. However, my theme is not mere antiquarianism. Moreover, this was a movement of youth — Stickney died at thirty, "Bay" Lodge at thirty-six, Moody at forty-one, and though Santayana is still living, he ceased to write poetry after his thirty-eighth year.

The first fact of importance is that pessimism was part of the problem of the group. They were aware of Schopenhauer, von Hartmann, Wagner, and Max Nordau. Lodge dedicates his youthful volume, *The Song of the Wave,* to Leopardi, quotes Leconte de Lisle, writes a poem to nothingness, and has two sonnets on Nirvana, which will come as a blessed release when "God grows mortal in men's hearts of stone." The best remembered poem of Santayana begins: "My heart rebels against my generation," and includes this striking passage:

> What would ye gain, ye seekers, with your striving,
> Or what vast Babel raise you on your shoulders?
> You multiply distresses, and your children
>   Surely will curse you.

Moody's *Gloucester Moors and Other Poems* compares the earth in space to a slave-ship:

> By her battened hatch I leaned and caught
> Sounds from the noisome hold, —
> Cursing and sighing of souls distraught
> And cries too sad to be told,

and exclaims:

> God, dear God! Does she know her port,
> Though she goes so far about?
> Or blind astray, does she make her sport
> To brazen and chance it out?

What is probably the most beautiful sonnet by Trumbull Stickney is a statement that life is illusion. With all

its old-fashioned rhetoric the poem still has its power
to charm:

> Be still. The Hanging Gardens were a dream
> That over Persian roses flew to kiss
> The curléd lashes of Semiramis.
> Troy never was, nor green Skamander stream.
> Provence and Troubadour are merest lies.
> The glorious hair of Venice was a beam
> Made within Titian's eye. The sunsets seem,
> The world is very old and nothing is.
> Be still. Thou foolish thing, thou canst not wake,
> Nor thy tears wedge thy soldered lids apart,
> But patter in the darkness of thy heart.
> Thy brain is plagued. Thou art a frighted owl
> Blind with the light of life thou'ldst not forsake,
> And Error loves and nourishes thy soul.

Associated with this pessimism is the sense that
Christianity is a failure, albeit a failure that still haunts
mankind. Thus Stickney entreats his readers to live in
the hour — the Lord who was the Future died a long
time ago. In a poem addressed to the Mater Dolorosa,
Lodge sympathizes with the Virgin's agony because the
sacrifice was vain, the image of Christ has crumbled,
the altar is empty, and the poet's unbelieving lips are
stone; and in a sonnet occasioned by the crucifixion he
pictures Jesus calling three times upon God the Father
without reply, and concludes:

> the great sweat beaded on His face,
> The vital sob urged outward, and a space
> Rose through dissolving faith the Eternal Lie!

To Moody, never so coarse-grained as these contemporaries, Christianity remained a perpetual perhaps. Two poems record personal experiences. In one, called "Good Friday Night," Christ seems to walk the road with the poet, but remains obstinately silent; in the other, "Second Coming," the poet catches a glimpse of a figure he thinks is Jesus bending over a Levantine sailor at work. This poem ends:

> Thine image gently fades from earth!
>   Thy churches are as empty shells,
> Dim-plaining of thy words and worth,
>   And of thy funerals!
> But oh, upon what errand, then,
>   Leanest thou at the sailor's ear?
> Hast thou yet more to say, that men
>   Have heard not, and must hear?

In his subtler prose treatise, *Poetry and Religion* (1900), Santayana generalizes this position, as he does in *Three Philosophical Poets* (1910). For him religion passes into poetry and disappears, as may be seen in this paragraph from the concluding chapter:

Take, for instance the doctrine of transubstantiation. A metaphor here is the basis of a dogma, because the dogma rises to the same subtle region as the metaphor, and gathers its sap from the same soil of emotion. Religion has here rediscovered its affinity with poetry, and in insisting on the truth of its mystery it unconsciously vindicates the ideality of its truth. Under the accidents of bread and wine lies, says the dogma, the substance of Christ's body, blood, and divinity. What is that but to treat facts as an appearance, and their ideal import as a reality? And to do this is the very essence of poetry, for which everything visible is a sacrament — an outward sign of that inward grace for which the soul is thirsting.

Later, in the volume called *Soliloquies in England* (1922), Santayana, while proclaiming in the prologue that "the human mind at best is a sort of song," was to remark that "Christ and Buddha are called saviours of the world; I think it must be in irony, for the world is just as much in need of salvation as ever. Death and insight and salvation are personal."

The poetry for which this philosopher made several grave and beautiful pleas appears among these young writers in two ways — in delight in life, sheer exuberance, a tingling consciousness of sensory existence, arising, I think, from the feeling that "death and insight and salvation are personal"; and in literary form. This delight quite contradicts their pessimism. Youthful vitality is strongest in Lodge — see, for example, "The Song of the Wave," despite its echoes of Henley and Kipling — and in William Vaughn Moody, in whom sensory pleasure passed into mystical insight. He wrote Daniel Gregory Mason in April, 1896, "I walk about in an amber clot of sensuousness, and feel the sap mount, like a tree," and six years later, in Greece, noted with approval that the Greeks taught "a doctrine of mystic regeneration to be achieved . . . not through denial of this life but by a complete entering it." A graphic example of sensory mystic experience appears in one of his letters:

Yesterday I was skating on a patch of ice in the park, under a poverty-stricken sky flying a pitiful flag of sunset. Some little muckers were guying a slim raw-boned Irish girl of fifteen, who circled and darted under their banter with complete unconcern. She was in the fledgling stage, all legs and arms, tall and adorably awkward, with a huge hat full of rusty feathers, thin skirts tucked up above spindling ankles, and a gay aplomb and swing in the body that was ravishing. We caught hands in midflight and skated for an hour, almost alone and quite silent, while the rag of sunset rotted to pieces. I have had few sensations in life that I would exchange for the warmth of her hand through the ragged glove, and the pathetic curve of the half-formed breast where the back of my wrist touched her body. I came away mystically shaken and elate. It is thus the angels converse. She was something absolutely authentic, new, and inexpressible, something which only nature could mix for the heart's intoxication, a compound of ragamuffin, pal, mistress, nun, sister, harlequin, outcast, and bird of God, — with something else bafflingly suffused, something ridiculous and frail and savage and tender. With a world offering such rencontres, such aery strifes and adventures, who would not live a thousand years stone dumb?

From a poet, of course, the last question is purely rhetorical, inasmuch as it was precisely to the explication of "something else bafflingly suffused," of "something ridiculous and frail and savage and tender" that Moody directed his most ambitious work, as, for that matter, did his three contemporaries.

Now that Wagner is old hat, it is hard for us to understand the revolutionary effect the handling of mythology in the *Ring* operas formerly possessed. This revolution becomes somewhat easier to comprehend when one remembers that the quasi-mythical poetic dramas of Ibsen — *Brand, Peer Gynt,* and *Emperor and Galilean* — were known in the nineties in advanced circles, and when one recalls the immense vogue of John Fiske, whose *Myths and Myth-Makers* (1872) had by no means been forgotten. Moreover, sociologists and anthropologists, still in the penumbra of the formulations of Herbert Spencer, were approaching comparative mythology as something more profound than literary lore; and, beginning in 1890, the magisterial work of Sir James Frazer, *The Golden Bough,* was being published. Young writers dissatisfied with orthodox belief and sensitive to new modes of cultural interpretation almost inevitably turned to myth as explanation and, almost as inevitably, cast their poems in masques, Greek dramas, or other forms permitting a large admixture of lyrical utterance to parallel, as it were, the Wagnerian music drama.

In 1904 George Cabot Lodge published *Cain: A Drama,* which is gravely dedicated "to the deathless memory of Jesus of Nazareth," and in 1908 *Herakles,* a play in twelve verbose scenes, the meaning of which is supposed to be made clear by an anonymous poet and an equally nameless woman, who, at the end of the drama, is gathered into the arms of Prometheus the fire-bringer. In 1902 Trumbull Stickney's volume, *Dramatic Verses,* culminated in *Prometheus Pyrphoros,* far more austere in tone and treatment than the plays

by Lodge. Santayana's *Lucifer; or, The Heavenly Truce*
first appeared in 1899 and was republished in 1924;
and his *The Hermit in Carmel* came out in 1901.
Moody's uncompleted trilogy began with *The Masque
of Judgment* in 1900, continued with *The Fire-Bringer*
in 1904, and would have concluded with *The Death of
Eve,* a fragment of which is contained in the *Poems and
Poetic Dramas* of 1912.

The characters of Santayana's *Lucifer* illustrate the
boldness of the mythological approach in these dramas.
They include Lucifer, Mephistopheles, and other figures
from Talmudic and Biblical legend; Zeus, Hermes, and
various gods and goddesses from Greece; the Risen
Christ, Michael, Saint Peter, and angels and saints from
Christian lore. In a preface which the mature philosopher wrote concerning the work of his youth, Santayana
declared, "I did not go in search of anything exotic;
these are my own Penates," indicated that he had no
occasion to apologize for the philosophy of the poem,
and sketched out a possible sequel in which Lucifer, like
Empedocles, should hurl himself into Aetna, so that
the substance of which he is composed "might somewhere contribute to a natural, happy, and pious life."
Lucifer is essentially an embodiment of modern self-
consciousness, rising superior to the medieval Christian
order, envying the wholeness of the pagan world, embodied in the charming figure of Hermes, but unable
to return to it, partly because, as a great concluding
speech of Zeus mournfully indicates, Zeus himself, to-

gether with the whole Olympic pantheon, is mortal. The doctrine is that of Lucretius; and at the end of the drama Lucifer, incarnation of modern self-consciousness, desires to return to the bosom of earth, even if it be to the stark, evolutionary universe of nineteenth-century physics:

> O ye hills that I have known of old,
> Unravished of the sun, ye snowy flock
> For ever sleeping, take me to your fold
> And in your flanks of adamantine rock
> Entomb my fiery heart. Over me spread
> Your frozen shroud and wreathe me in ice-flowers,
> To watch with you through everlasting hours
> And not remember.

The error of Lucifer, Santayana tells us, is to assume that, like the modern artist, he has an absolute vision of truth. "Spirit," wrote the author twenty-five years after his play was completed,

is sustained and inspired at every point by a substance at work beneath or above it; a substance also the source of every other spirit, and of all the influences and conventions in which spirit is entangled. The autonomy of spirit is spiritual only and no excuse for rebellion against the accidents that create it or that create a different spirit elsewhere . . . Lucifer . . . has sterilized his roots; and what may still melt him is not a fresh illusion of life for himself, but only the ideal charm of another [that is, Hermes] which, being still unsevered from its soil, can be beautiful and happy. This fragrance of nature, borne upon a passing wind, is at once blown away again; it has no power to reknit the bonds by which Lucifer's mind was attached to its own substance. He must fall back, wretched but self-justified, on the absolute claims of his living thought. On his own thought, and by it, as he sadly believes, all things are painted.

The sense of despair which seems to overcome writers like Fitzgerald and Hart Crane is here described in philosophic terms and in noble poetic utterance, and it is precisely in the rebellious "autonomy of spirit," the failure to attach one's self to earth, to religious belief, or to philosophic tradition, that Santayana locates the impulse to destruction evident in the moderns. Says Lucifer, in the last scene:

> To die is better than to live. Our sin
> Alone is fertile, peopling all the earth
> With lust and error and their troublous kin,

and he says this because he has been the occasion of the death of Hermes, the perfect embodiment of youth and art. The enigma of the bright Medusa is here translated out of aesthetic into philosophic terms.

But though Lucifer luxuriates in mythological figures, they are rather a form of poetic shorthand than products of that intuitive assent which alone gives meaning to myth; and the play, furthermore, requires allegiance to Santayana's special philosophy for its full meaning — the philosophy set forth in the five volumes of *The Life of Reason*. I therefore turn to William Vaughn Moody.

V

Like writers in the twenties and thirties Moody was
thoroughly at odds with the industrial order. He found
the academic world sterile — at every lecture, he said,
I slay a poet — and by and by he quit it. He had to
brace himself to endure Chicago — the enervating thing
about the place is its shallow kindness, he wrote.
"Gloucester Moors" is a poem of moral indignation;
"Jetsam" denounces the factory system; "The Brute"
is as angry a statement as, in another genre, is Dos
Passos's *U.S.A.* The two great odes — "In Time of
Hesitation" and "On A Soldier Fallen in the Philip-
pines" — excoriate foreign policy in a spirit of lofty
scorn forming the substratum for that enigmatic poem
"The Quarry," which pictures Asia as a snow-white
elephant dogged by beasts of prey, an eagle also in
pursuit. Mr. David Henry, in his study, points out that
in "I am the Woman" Moody summed up all the rebellious feminism of Meredith, Shaw, H. G. Wells, and
others. Moody told Ferdinand Schevill that *The Masque
of Judgment* was to be "a kind of Hebrew Götterdämmerung, with a chance for some real speaking-out-in-
meeting," and he made the central figures of his trilogy
the three arch-rebels, Prometheus, Raphael, and Eve.
Nevertheless, it is not on the rebellious, but on the
affirmative side that I approach him.

In New York where

> the town flings down
> Its lust by day for its nightly lust,

Moody once wrote a poem about an Italian street-singer whose pagan voice is an ironical comment on the competitive order. The poem concludes:

> Heart, we have chosen the better part!
> Save sacred love and sacred art
> Nothing is good for long.

Love and art, however, are sacred in no religious or theological sense, but only in the sense that they have, when deeply experienced, a consecration of their own. Here, once more, is our familiar theme. What does Moody do with it?

He tries to develop its universal meaning in terms of universal mythology — Greek in *The Fire-Bringer,* Christian in *The Masque of Judgment,* Hebraic in the unfinished *Death of Eve.* Art and love are sacred so long as God and man are mutually dependent. When man rebels against God, as in *The Fire-Bringer,* the result is a splendor of sensuous life, but it is nothing more than sensuous life, as, at the end of that drama, a chorus of young men drown the voice of Pandora:

> Eros, how sweet
> Is the cup of thy drunkenness!
> Dionysus, how our feet
> Hasten to the burning cup
> Thou liftest up!
> But O how sweetest and how most burning it is
> To drink of the wine of thy lightsome chalices,
> Apollo! Apollo! To-day
> We say we will follow thee and put all others away.

For thou alone, O thou alone art he
Who settest the imprisoned spirit free,
And sometimes leadest the rapt soul on
Where never mortal thought has gone;
Till by the ultimate stream
Of vision and of dream
She stands
With startled eyes and outstretched hands,
Looking where other suns rise over other lands,
And rends the lonely skies with her prophetic
    scream.

Love, enthusiasm, art will take you far, but only to the
boundary of the unknown.

In *The Masque of Judgment,* earlier written but
second in the intellectual order, this situation is reversed.
The shock of recognition which occasioned the composition of the drama was a Venetian triptych representing
the Last Judgment, a picture which stung Moody to
the quick, indignant that God could so treat the
creation that He loved. The setting is suggested by the
Dolomite Alps, the language is occasionally reminiscent
of Milton and the theme is, in a sense, opposed to that
of *Paradise Lost,* since Moody seeks to justify the ways of
man to God. A series of mysterious figures, in part
gleaned from the Book of Revelations and locked in
even more mysterious combat, gives veiled warning to
God of the disaster to heaven that will follow upon the
destruction of earth, but though Moody is fair to parts
of the Christian story — for example, the wonderful
hymn of the Redeemed Spirits, which begins:

In the wilds of life astray,
Held far from our delight,
Following the cloud by day
And the fire by night,
Came we a desert way.
O Lord, with apples feed us,
With flagons stay!
By Thy still waters lead us! —

the life of heaven dims, the angels and the lamps about God's throne grow grey and aged, and the Worm that never dies gnaws at the bastions of the celestial walls. The meaning is virtually Hegelian. In a concluding speech Raphael, who is Moody's *raisonneur* in the poem, says of God:

Would He had dared
To nerve each member of his mighty frame —
Man, beast, and tree, and all the shapes of will
That dream their darling ends in clod and star —
To everlasting conflict, wringing peace
From struggle and from struggle peace again,
Higher and sweeter and more passionate
With every danger passed! Would He had spared
That dark Antagonist whose enmity
Gave Him rejoicing sinews, for of Him
His foe was flesh of flesh and bone of bone,
With suicidal hand He smote him down,
And now indeed His lethal pangs begin.

For Moody, God severed from man — that is, from His sentient creation — became like Thomas Hardy's deity, a godhead dying downward from the brain.

How, then, were the severed halves of the universe to be once more fused? How were God the Creator and man the creation to be reunited in the third member of the trilogy? We do not know, for we have only one act of *The Death of Eve,* in which, after aeons of ages, Eve and her son Cain, emblem of human misfortune, re-enter the gate of the Garden of Eden. However, there also exist certain passages in Moody's letters, a narrative poem entitled "The Death of Eve," and Pandora's prophetic lyric in *The Fire-Bringer,* all of which illumine Moody's intention in bringing the oldest of Biblical legends to bear upon the eschatological problem of *The Masque of Judgment.* In *The Fire-Bringer* Moody transformed Pandora from the embodiment of that curiosity which brought misery upon mankind into a vessel of intuitive wisdom; so, likewise, he planned to make Eve, the traditional occasion of man's tragedy, the instrument of man's reconciliation. Pandora's matchless lyric in *The Fire-Bringer* expresses the philosophic mode of this reconciliation; and "Eve's Song," part of the narrative poem, "The Death of Eve," expresses its mystical possibility. Here is Pandora's song:

> I stood within the heart of God;
> It seemed a place that I had known:
> (I was blood-sister to the clod,
> Blood-brother to the stone.)

> I found my love and labor there,
> My house, my raiment, meat and wine,
> My ancient rage, my old despair, —
> Yea, all things that were mine.

I saw the spring and summer pass,
The trees grow bare, and winter come;
All was the same as once it was
Upon my hills at home.

Then suddenly in my own heart
I felt God walk and gaze about;
He spoke; his words seemed held apart
With gladness and with doubt.

"Here is my meat and wine," He said,
"My love, my toil, my ancient care;
Here is my cloak, my book, my bed,
And here my old despair.

"Here are my seasons: winter, spring,
Summer the same, and autumn spills
The fruits I look for; everything
As on my heavenly hills."

According to Mrs. Moody the trilogy was to have concluded with a "lyric murmur of pure human joy, based
upon . . . consciousness of mutual life," the sense of
renewal in the world after Eve's song of reconciliation.
The song by Eve which we have in the narrative poem
is too long to quote, but some glimpse of Moody's intention may be gleaned from two stanzas:

Behold, against thy will, against thy word,
Against the wrath and warning of thy sword,
Eve has been Eve, O Lord!
A pitcher filled, she comes back from the brook,
A wain she comes, laden with mellow ears;
She is a roll inscribed, a prophet's book
Writ strong with characters.
Behold, Eve willed it so; look, if it be so, look!
· · · · · · · · · · · · · ·

> Herself hath searched her softly through and
>   through;
> Singing she lifts her full soul up to view;
> Lord, do Thou praise it, too!
> Look, as she turns it, how it dartles free
> Its gathered meanings: woman, mother, wife,
> Spirit that was and is and waits to be,
> Worm of the dust of life,
> Child, sister — ghostly rays! What lights are these,
>   Lord, see!

I take the meaning of this to be that the curve of human experience cannot be fulfilled until, through the patience of love, the human being intuitively grasps the truth that matter and sex, the life of possession and the life of the senses do in the long run depend for their value upon the life of the spirit, a phrase our contemporaries are unwilling to utter.

We must allow Moody to write in his own time and within the conventions of that time. Yet a recent history of American poetry begins its discussion of his work by saying that the present reader of his verse "is almost certain to be faced with embarrassment." I do not feel in the least embarrassed in reading him, and it seems to me the phrase points up a certain temporal parochialism in contemporary criticism. But whether one accepts his poetry or not, the trilogy, which depends, as Rossetti said poetry should depend, upon fundamental brain-work for its execution and its interpretation, indicates that the writer cannot possibly long exist in a merely biological world. So far as I can remember, no literary period previous to ours has tried to establish the autonomy of art on the premise that the world of the spirit has vanished. The lonely writer of our time, however, having denied religion and having severed himself from virtually every other traditional function of the artist, is too often trying to produce an entire universe of discourse out of his own consciousness, and that is why, it seems to me, he burns himself out too quickly and too young. He is not only in revolt against God and against society, he is in revolt against the nature of art itself. Possibly Moody's modernization of myth did not succeed; clearly, however, he was content to appeal to universal myth rather than to the private myths of the subconscious or the unconscious, and in his large discourse, even if it be set down as failure (and I do not think it is a failure), he suggests that if there be such a thing as an autonomy of art, art is autonomous only as a province within the larger empire of human history and of human experience.

3

THE *Radical*

I have made Scott Fitzgerald's *This Side of Paradise* the occasion, though not the subject, of these discourses because of the typicality of its theme. That theme is the revolt of youth in the name of art against contemporary culture. Because the existing order did not give Amory Blaine scope for his aesthetic perceptions and his emotional desires, he found love, business, politics, and religion futile, and at the end of the novel falls back upon himself for the meaning of existence. This attitude, far more maturely expressed, became the attitude of many writers in the twenties and since. I have suggested that it lies at the bottom of such novels as *The Enormous Room, Three Soldiers, Main Street,* and *Look Homeward, Angel.* Almost any anthology of recent and contemporary American poetry reveals the continuance of a solipsistic philosophy. For example, in Oscar Williams' excellent *Little Treasury of American*

Poetry (1948), the final poem, by Marguerite Young, entitled "Speculative Evening," is, if I understand it rightly, an exercise in transcendental solitude:

> If there were no past, but specious present
>   only, if twinkle ago
> By the edict of a heavenly geometer
> Had been created this earth of pointed fir
>   trees, December snow,
> Jewel eye, yet who would realize the
>   colossal joke?
>
> For with our equipment of memory,
> Yet would this present seem entire fragment
>   and whole
> To sailor, soul, spectator of storms, and all
>   would be
> Exactly clouded, and the snow goose put on
>   white at its maturity
> And the albino crow who gets no partner in
>   mortal marriage
> Would tap at the window in surf among red
>   berries,
> And I myself would feel my crucial age
> And cry for ambassadors like dolls among
>   the wrinkled stars.
>
> And I, poor pensioner in nature's house
> In smoky beams of evening's blowing light
> Would behold fallacious futures, impermanence
>   of fact, brightest of all stars, Sirius,
> And harpers harping on a sea of glass.

This seems to say that the Berkeleian world of the knife-edge present is, to the poet, a "poor pensioner in nature's house," all that is, including as it does both a fallacious future and impermanent facts. A similar identification of the ego with the universe can be discovered in poems like Muriel Rukeyser's "Ajanta," Delmore Schwartz's "In the Naked Bed, in Plato's Cave," Conrad Aiken's *Senlin*, and "The Man with the Blue Guitar" of Wallace Stevens, to name only familiar examples. In thus categorizing these poems I am, of course, merely making a statement about them, I am not inferring invidious comparisons with other poetry or other philosophies. And to characterize the allure of the theory that the artist, be he painter, poet, or musician, is in possession of some special and private sort of truth, to which, though it slay him, he is to sacrifice, if necessary, other sorts of truth — for example, the truth of economics, or the truth of patriotism, the truth of ethics, or the truth of science — I have borrowed from Willa Cather's memorable title, *Youth and the Bright Medusa*.

It is my contention, among other matters, that this revolt of youth in the name of art is rather older than youth likes to believe, and that the revolt of the twenties in particular was culmination rather than beginning. In my first lecture I analyzed, especially in the case of Miss Cather's fiction, the modern writer's concept of the growth of the artist toward expression, a well-nigh mystical shaping of personality until it becomes the special conduit of something known as truth in art. Yet the contemporary artist, the poet in particular, having cast off traditional belief and having also lost the hampering, yet formative, influence of status in a society which denies him the support due to the priest and the patronage due from the aristocrat, faces a dilemma in communicating this truth. If he projects his private psychical experience upon the world, his symbols are likely to be so unintelligible as to bring him perilously close to talking to himself. The point can be quickly illustrated. In *The New Statesman and Nation* for January 12, 1952, reviewing a book by C. Handley-Read on the art of Wyndham Lewis, the reviewer presented his readers with this kind of "interpretation":

All this is clear indication that Mr. Lewis's whole approach (to form, to composition, to design — and "composition" is design in depth) is that of linear drawing — the lines of the *outlines* of forms predominating. Not all drawing is linear, of course; volume and even profile may be expressed without recourse to an outlining line; indeed, volume is most precisely indicated by a species of scribble. But for Mr. Lewis it is outline, alternating rhythmically between concave and convex, which provides him with the method by which forms, either related or in isolation, are evoked. What sense of mass there is is conveyed by the sharp edges of a form rather than by its "infilling,"[1] to use Mr. Handley-Read's word. "Infilling" is invariably less expressive than silhouette in Mr. Lewis's work: the middles of his shapes often lack thrust or direction, are dead in texture and neutral in tone. But their fringes, their *drawn* edges are, on the other hand, always expressive. They gesticulate. And in this Mr. Lewis is the opposite of a Cubist:

---

[1] And a most unfortunate word it is, with its echo of *Einfühlung*, which means something quite different. Why not "filling in"?

the Cubist begins with the "infilling" — the sensation of a plane — and proceeds outwards, to find the outline: Mr. Lewis finds the outline first. Indeed, he finds it too soon.

My point is not to deny subtlety to art criticism of this order, but it is criticism which says nothing to the general reader, it is in no sense public discourse, and this talk of fringes that "gesticulate," of outlines discovered "too soon," of the precision of "scribble," the inadequacies of an "outlining" line (what other kinds of line are there?), and of shapes having middles that lack "thrust" or "direction" is talk in a private universe of discourse that has little to do with the discourse of Sir Joshua Reynolds or of writers like Reinach, Burckhardt, or Bosanquet.

The old subject matter being abandoned, intelligible public discourse through art or about art becomes an increasingly difficult bravura problem in technological discourse designed to be as unintelligible to the lay public as is necessarily the technological discourse of engineering, medicine, or nuclear physics.

The modern artist, the modern writer, or the modern critic, in casting about for some publicly acceptable, yet novel set of symbols he can use as aesthetic logic, turns sometimes to myth. We have examined virtually the last group of American poets to work creatively with traditional myth. Since their time not even the acceptance of Freud and Jung nor the popularity of anthropology has evolved a general cultural surrogate for the Biblical cosmogony of Milton or for the gods of ancient Hellas.

This seems at first a merely academic observation. It is, however, of deep intellectual significance, as may be seen in modernism elsewhere — for example, in France. André Gide was, I take it, the great representative figure in contemporary French writing, a modern of moderns, and, in the judgment of some critics, the representative European modern writer *par excellence.* Yet, as a glance at the titles of his works will show, classical myth and Biblical reference are the very marrow of his bones. He calls his books after Oedipus, Theseus, Narcissus, Prometheus, Philoctetes, Candaules, Corydon, and Persephone; or he entitles them *The Return of the Prodigal,* or *Strait Is the Gate.* He writes of these symbolic themes as no contemporary American would write; or, to speak more accurately, he writes of himself apropos of these traditional symbols, confident that in using them he will establish an immediate connection with the culture of his readers. A great confessional library takes on the depth and richness created by the accumulated human experience evoked by these mythical names, and, moreover, an enormous burden of explanation is lifted from the writer by their use. But the American is without the help of this traditional pattern because we have now neither a classical nor a Biblical culture.

The repudiation or lack of these common symbols and of what, for want of a better phrase, I may call public subject matter, has thrown a burden upon contemporary art greater than it should bear. In losing status and in repudiating tradition, the contemporary craftsman has also come to doubt whether art has its necessary grammar; or, if he cannot wholly avoid the grammatical problem, he minimizes it in proportion as the truth of grammar substantiates the truth of traditional forms. If you ask a disciple of Schönberg, Why the twelve-tone scale? he is likely to retort: Why not? If you ask whether the pleasure to be gained from *Finnegans Wake* is in proportion to the trouble of unraveling it, the new criticism responds that Joyce's prose lies beyond the pleasure principle. If you admit that there is distortion in figure painting all the way from Byzantium to the Varga girl but protest that painting which is all distortion destroys the aesthetic pleasure of measuring what is distorted against what is normal, the painter looks baffled, or says helplessly: "Well, that's the way I saw it." There is a kind of defiant irreconcilability between the private universe of individual artists and the usual assumption that the conventions of any art represent a useful compromise between the demands of creation and the demands of the percipient audience. The artist, especially the younger artist, dramatizes himself as a root-and-branch rebel and might conceivably quote scripture to his purpose: "Behold I make all things new." He becomes, in short, the radical. His radicalism is, or might be, part of a sound and healthy American cultural tradition. The difficulty is to define the quality of this radicalism in American art.

II

We may begin by noting the virtual lack in our cultural history of a radical American aesthetic. With some exceptions — the prosody of Whitman, American jazz, and the skyscraper are, perhaps, examples — the theory and practice of art in America, so far as radicalism is concerned, are a history of adaptation. Cubism, pointillism, impressionism, symbolism, romanticism, realism, futurism, Freudianism — if these or other terms represent, or have represented, rebellion in the arts, they have originated with monotonous regularity outside the United States. They have sometimes been adapted to local conditions in such a way as to disguise their parentage in part, but even in the case of the three exceptions I listed, a purely American origin is at least doubtful. The skyscraper, and, for that matter, the architectural innovations of so brilliant a modern as Frank Lloyd Wright, had their precedents in iron-and-glass construction in Victorian England, in Japanese architecture, and in the design of ocean-going vessels like the "Great Eastern," and form part of what is known as the international style. Jazz is more characteristically American, but its origins lie, at least partially, in Afro-American rhythms and the cadences and harmonies of Wesleyan gospel hymns. Walt Whitman's chant owes something to the King James Bible, something to Italian opera, and something to Macpherson's Ossian, just as his poetic theory owes something to George Sand and Victor Hugo. Possibly indebtednesses like these are the normal obligations which posterity owes to its ancestors — I do not press the point and am content to regard Whitman, Wright, and W. C. Handy as radical innovators; still, the general proposition stands that we have been adapters of European radicalisms in the fine arts more often than we have been self-originating rebels. But to this general rule there is one notable exception: the theory of the status of the arts, especially the art of literature, to the republic.

I have tried to work out the genesis and history of this principle in a book called *The Theory of American Literature,* published a few years ago. Briefly, the principle was that a new nation established on true, philosophic lines must infallibly produce a new and virtuous culture, including the arts. On the one hand, this theory meant as distinct a repudiation of much of the cultural past as, to cite a more modern instance, the repudiation of so-called bourgeois literature by Soviet Russia; and on the other hand, it meant that the writer ought constantly to recur to the theory of republican art under a republican form of government. The repudiation of Europe, which is the note of this theory, begins early — for example, Timothy Dwight, in 1794, wrote this:

> Look not to Europe, for examples just
> Of order, manners, customs, doctrines, laws,
> Of happiness, or virtue . . . .
>   Change, but change alone,
> By wise improvement of thy blessings rare:
> And copy not from others. Shun the lures
> Of Europe.

Emerson's famous dictum that we have listened too long
to the courtly muses of Europe, like Whitman's repudiation of "feudalism," is not mere chauvinism, it is the
expression of the theory that, the republic being founded
on true, radical, and philosophic lines, nothing less than
a radical alteration in the traditional themes of literature will express its cultural life. Titles like *America:
The Permanent Revolution* and phrases like "Europe is
washed up" still retain this implication. The same note
recurs even in Henry James, in whom the moral
superiority of naive Americans over more worldly or
more decadent Europeans is a continuing theme.

All this is nothing novel, nothing strange. But the
other half of the equation — the doctrine that the
writer ought constantly to recur to republican principles,
even at the cost of being thought "radical" — leads us
into controversial territory. The relative thinness of the
American muse in works of pure imagination is offset
by the richness of her products as works on public
issues. Even in the case of Poe, our principal exhibit as
pure romanticism, an astonishing amount of his prose
is devoted to a conservative exploration of republican
theory; and memorable work by Franklin, Freneau,
Paine, Jefferson, Emerson, Thoreau, Whittier, Lowell,
Whitman, Mark Twain, Howells, Henry Adams, and
others centers in notable degree upon public contro-
versies arising from the failure of the great republic
to live up to its own premises. That failure might
present itself to the writer as a dangerous recrudescence

of monarchial principles disguised as federalism, or as the failure to abolish the undemocratic institution of slavery, or as the conquest of the republic by the money power, or as the confusion of democracy with demagoguery — the point of works as scattered in time as Brackenridge's *Modern Chivalry,* Melville's *Mardi,* Henry Adams' *Democracy,* and Robert Penn Warren's *All the King's Men.*

I am far from saying that all American men of letters are radical—I should stub my toe on Washington Irving, if I did; and, of course, radicalism is relative to time and occasion. Thus, most of us accept as radical in its place Huck Finn's decision to go to hell rather than return Nigger Jim to slavery, but we are also likely to feel that Sinclair Lewis' attack on fascism in *It Can't Happen Here* is dated, though both books spring from that unreasonable, persistent, and radical concept of the dignity of the individual we like to equate with an American philosophy. By and large, however, our great men of literature have been too often a race of rebels for us to ignore this overriding characteristic in American literary history; and it is the recognition of this truth that permited Granville Hicks, then in his communistic phase, to write *The Great Tradition,* an interpretation of American literary development which equated this rebelliousness with Marxism. Unfortunately for the theory, most of the writers in question had never heard of Marx or never studied him; but what is more important, the radicalism at the root of the

literary tradition I am talking about is quite other than
the radicalism popularly associated with the Communist
party. It is, indeed, one of the queer results of the siege
mentality from which the nation is today suffering that,
before getting back to Scott Fitzgerald, his contemporaries and successors, I find this roundabout digres-
sion necessary to my theme.

Such are the pressures of conformity today that
"radical" is no longer a respectable word. A radical is
a red, and a red is either a communist, a crypto-com-
munist, or a fellow traveller. That there has been traditionally a totally different sort of radicalism in our
culture is something the pressures of the time are not
prepared to admit. Under present laws and present
customs, which do not distinguish between communism
and non-conformity, though these two attitudes are as
far apart as one pole is from another, a great many of
our most distinguished men of letters, were they alive
today, would be either silenced or in jail. Deviations
from conformity have driven artists off the air, off the
screen, and out of print. Any one who has had any
traffic lately with writing for the popular magazines is
witness to the hypersensitivity of these journals to any
variation from the current interpretation of Americanism. For the first time in our history — with, perhaps,
the doubtful exception of the period of the Alien and
Sedition laws — we have no radical writers, we have
no influential movement of protest, and we have, at
least for the moment, no important experimental move-

ment in any of the arts. A great and vital part of the American tradition has been estopped because of the substitution of something called "Americanism" for that constant recurrence to republican principles which I have defined as historically valid American radicalism. In proportion as we make our universities, our radio and other mass mediums, our newspapers, and our publishing houses, instruments of conformity, we inhibit ourselves inevitably from continuing the great literary tradition which gave us Whitman, Melville, Thoreau, Emerson, the elder Henry James, and even Whittier, William Cullen Bryant, and Oliver Wendell Holmes.

III

As I may not even now have made clear my notion of the American radical tradition, and since it is extremely important in this situation that I shall be clear, I turn to another field and appeal to educational rather than to aesthetic authority. In 1943 the president of Harvard University published in the *Atlantic Monthly* an article entitled: "Wanted: American Radicals," which, though it fluttered the dovecotes in certain alumni clubs, seemed to me then, and seems to me now, an admirable exposition of what American radicalism essentially ought to be. Mr. Conant noted that both the American liberal and the American conservative had virtually disappeared, that thought about public issues was either reactionary or radical, that both these camps have their origins in nineteenth-century Europe, and that he would like to hear a third vote in the republic — the voice of the American radical. The American radical, he said, springs from American soil and is firm in the belief that every man is as good as his neighbor and is entitled to a real chance in the world. He combines impracticality and common sense, applying to change the pragmatic question: Does it work?

The American radical believes in equality of opportunity, though not of awards, and is so violently opposed to inherited privilege that he might want to confiscate property by constitutional means every generation or so. He favors public education, but he fears federal control of institutions concerned with youth. He will try to decentralize the government and do what he can to rehabilitate local government, but when federal action proves necessary to maintain real freedom, he will call upon it, always placing individual rights above the police power of the state. He will fight against the sleeping sickness of nostalgia — the weakness of American public thought; he will be old-fashioned enough to believe in individual integrity, he will be hostile to current methods of advertising and sales promotion, since "The waves of distorted facts and beguiling half-truths with which our eyes and ears are daily saturated" form "one of the most insidious maladies of the age"; and, above all and quintessentially, he will be filled with individual contrariness, so that business and labor — and I add, on my own account, his own government —

will look upon him with profound suspicion. I quote
this paragraph:

The fundamental philosophy of the American radical is a
threat to much of the present leadership of both capital and
labor. For his equalitarian doctrine, if only partially successful, would change the complexion of the struggle between
management and labor. And this is the crux of his contribu-
tion to the current scene. He would use the powers of government to re-order the "haves and have-nots" every
generation to give flux to our social order. And given a high
degree of social mobility in America — a degree comparable
to that in a pioneer community of a century ago — labor
leaders would often find themselves negotiating with their
blood relations. If at the same time ownership and management of industry rarely if ever were passed on by inheritance,
nepotism or patronage, many aspects of the current industrial
picture would indeed be radically altered — altered in a
characteristically American way.

Mr. Conant's article is now almost ten years old, and
he did not, while thus beautifully defining the American
radical, say that he agreed with him, but the essay
springs from an understanding of the American tradition, which far transcends the current cry for Americanism — meaning by that much abused term a timor-
ous conformity.

IV

As I now may seem to have drifted from my principal theme, I remind you that at the end of *This Side
of Paradise* Amory Blaine delivers a boyish lecture on

socialism to three or four businessmen. We may accept this episode as a symbolic act, partly flowering in Fitzgerald's sociological disillusion about the rich, of whom he later said (in *All the Sad Young Men,* 1926):

They are different from you and me. They possess and enjoy early and it does something to them, makes them soft where we are hard, and cynical where we are trustful, in a way that, unless you were born rich, it is very difficult to understand. They think, deep in their hearts, that they are better than we are because we had to discover the compensations and refuges of life for ourselves.

This famous paragraph is in one sense not important, since, by refusing to follow it through, Fitzgerald failed to stiffen his fiction into the kind of social criticism Howells or Dreiser represents. But in identifying the reader, not with the rich, but with an undefined outgroup at cross purposes with wealth, and in looking at the rich with eyes at once scornful and tender, Fitzgerald again typifies the revolt of youth, this time against social and cultural environment.

This revolt, however, was not, as current comment tends to assume, a unique function of postwar disillusionment, but a recurrent American attitude. There was a youth movement, for example, at the end of the eighteenth century, which took shape as the Connecticut Wits; there was another in the forties of the last century — what Emerson called the "Newness" and what the political historians called the "Young America" movement; and there was a third — one which particularly concerns us — in the opening years of the twentieth century.

A poet like William Vaughn Moody, whom I have discussed, expresses this mood of youthful rebellion against materialist culture in a poem like "The Brute." The mood there set forth —

> "Till the mills I grind have ceased,
> The riches shall be dust of dust, dry ashes
> be the feast!" —

originated, I take it, in the profound discontent of the nineties with social and economic maladjustment. By 1912 this discontent had taken shape as the Bull Moose party and the "New Freedom" of Woodrow Wilson. In his first inaugural address Wilson, in a single sentence, phrased both the political and literary aspects of this movement, when he said:

We have been proud of our industrial achievements, but we have not hitherto stopped thoughtfully enough to count the cost, the cost of lives snuffed out, of energies overtaxed and broken, the fearful physical and spiritual cost to the men and women and children upon whom the dead weight and burden of it all has fallen pitilessly the years through.

What Wilson thus phrased had been the theme of a library of fiction by novelists like Robert Herrick, Winston Churchill, Brand Whitlock, Ernest Poole, and others; now, more significantly, by the second decade of the century, dissatisfaction with economic maladjustment had fused among the younger men into dissatisfaction with the accompanying cultural pattern, that genteel tradition which Santayana was to inter in 1931. The younger generation was shortly to capture *The Dial,* it was to found *The New Republic,* it was to create that short-lived but fascinating periodical, *The Seven Arts,* and it was to fill *The Masses,* suppressed by the government in 1917, with some of the finest black-and-white work of the century.

It would require another Emerson describing another Chardon Street Convention or discussing "Man, the Reformer," adequately to recreate the tingling excitement of that time. Herbert Croly and Walter Lippmann were reorienting the Jeffersonian and Hamiltonian traditions in works like *A Preface to Politics* and *The Promise of American Life.* In 1912 James Harvey Robinson was outlining the new theory of history in his volume by this name. That same year *Poetry: A Magazine of Verse* was born, with Ezra Pound, briefly, as foreign correspondent. Robert Frost's first book came out in 1913, the year of Lindsay's *General William Booth Enters into Heaven; The Spoon River Anthology* appeared in 1915, and in 1916 *Chicago Poems.* In 1914 Mencken, Nathan, and Willard Huntington Wright took over *The Smart Set,* and that year Spingarn announced that the new criticism had cut all connection with Matthew Arnold and the past, and was to devote itself to being creative.

The Armory Show of 1913 marked the revolt of the new painting against representational art, and meanwhile, at 291 Fifth Avenue, Alfred Stieglitz was remaking photography and exhibiting Cezanne, Matisse, Brancusi, and other Europeans along with Steichen, Marin, Max Weber, and younger Americans. In music one heard Gilbert's "Comedy Overture on Negro Themes" in 1910, the year of the beginning of the MacDowell Festivals at Peterborough; in 1911 Horatio W. Parker's *Mona* was performed at the Metropolitan; in 1915 John Alden Carpenter's "Adventures in a Perambulator" was played by the Chicago Symphony Orchestra; and by the end of the decade music by Griffes, Sowerby, Arthur Farwell, and others among the first wave of American modernists was vying for place on programs with the music of Schönberg and Prokofiev. *The Dial,* in 1917, affirmed that its spirit was to be "freely experimental, skeptical of inherited values, ready to examine old dogmas, and to submit afresh its sanctions to the test of experience," and by January, 1918, Robert Herrick was ready to assert that "we pass into a new world of self-consciousness" and out of the old world forever.

Everywhere the accent was on youth, youth aroused and militant against tradition and its elders. When a Catholic priest protested that Ibsen's plays were unfit for young girls, *The New Republic* told him that Ibsen was already outmoded and demanded a "new liberation" "more joyous as well as relentlessly rational" for the United States. Youth here, complained Randolph Bourne in an article on "The Cult of the Best," is crushed by tradition; he demanded colleges in which "men and women, in the fire of their youth, with conflicts and idealisms, questions and ambitions and desire for expression, come to serve an apprenticeship under the masters of the time." Youth, *The Dial* asserted in 1914, faces not only the usual handicaps, but also a well-supported taboo in the publishing houses: as one of the younger men said, "It is not that we have nothing to say, or that we do not know how to say it. It is that we have no place in which to say it." Progressivism, observed Frederick Ogg in 1915, is committed to nothing less than a "drastic reorganization of the American political and economic system." "Youth," lamented H. W. Boynton in 1916, "is no longer the Young Person," but "humanity in the ascendant, the ruling power, which has a right to know what sort of world it is set to rule over."

The amusing impudence of Max Otto's figurative language in describing the orthodox college course in philosophy while reviewing John Dewey's *Creative Intelligence* (1917) is equally illuminating. In *The Dial* he writes:

The orthodox course in philosophy is a drama in three acts. In the first act the student is kidnapped by the professor and imprisoned in a cave. Communication with anything or anybody outside is demonstrated by the captor to be impossible. Between the student and the world he lately occupied obtrudes the impassable wall of subjectivity. With the aid of the bull's eye supplied by the professor, every recess of the

The second act is given over to the dramatic rescue of the prisoner. The professor and a few accomplices know of a subterranean passage! Through this they lead the way out of the cave. But, alas, there is no joy in the new freedom, for the world into which the student is released is not a living appealing world. It is to the green earth whence he was snatched as paper flowers are to the rose.

Hereupon follows the third act, in which the student gradually awakes. He discovers that there has been no real kidnapping and consequently no rescue; that nothing indeed has happened excepting that his credulity has been imposed upon. The conclusion of the drama depends upon the individual student's sense of humor, but, at all events, there comes to be a hollow sound to the phrase, "Philosophy, the guide of life."

This disrespectful treatment of metaphysical tradition was possible because of the general conviction that the youth of America, the youth of France, the youth of India, the youth of Japan, all of whom (and others) had articles devoted to them, were capable of "taking over" since they were "still young enough in spirit to harbor generous hopes for . . . civilization." Two final citations from the year 1918 will drive home the point.

One is a poem in *The Dial,* entitled "The Young World," by James Oppenheim, a mystical celebration of world-wide youthful rebellion in the name, so to speak, of the Great Society of Josiah Royce. Here are parts of the poem:

These youngsters are aliens and exiles among
    their parents:
Where they go
Goes rebellion . . . .

O what is the word
Burning in the heart of youth?
Is it the word, God?
Is it the word, Fatherland?
Is it the word, Liberty?
It is none of these words: the word
Has not been shaped, has not
Pealed its bugle-challenge on Earth.

(Observe, again, the idea of the mystical initiate, the
Davidsbündler motif.)

Are you artists, O spirits of the young world?
Are you those who seek to transform destroying
    things
Into symbols of glory and works of fruitfulness?
Would you end war, clean out poverty, stop
    disease?
Neither law nor science shall suffice,
But only Art.

. . . .

Not unions, commissions, and societies
Organized for a common gain,
But the natural coming of a few together
Like fragments flying into place
To make a new personality
Larger than a single man.

This, the poem concludes, is the "divine brotherhood
of the young."

The other exhibit is an article by Van Wyck Brooks, then just over thirty, occasioned by a book by Pierre de Lanux entitled *Young France and New America* (1918). The theme of the work, says Brooks in *The Dial,* is: "A conquest of the world by young people of all nations, the sloughing off of the old skin of society," and this, he thinks, will result in "the fullest and the freest expression of every people along the lines of its own genius." In America we must erase the "weary, baffled expression one sees in so many . . . middle-aged American faces," we must give ourselves over to the younger generation. Why?

How many drafts we have issued in the past upon European thought, unbalanced by any investment of our own! The younger generation have come to feel this obligation acutely. At the same time they have been taught to speak a certain language in common by the social movements of the last twenty years. . . . They see that we Americans have never so much as dreamed of a radically more beautiful civilization, our Utopias having been so generally of the nature of Edward Bellamy's, complex and ingenious mechanisms, liberating the soul into a vacuum of ennui. They see that it is art and literature which give the soul its higher values, and make life worthy of intercession, and that every effective social revolution has been led up to and inspired by visionary leaders who have shown men what they might become and what they miss in living as they do. . . .

Certainly no true social revolution will ever be possible in this country till a race of artists, profound and sincere, have brought us face to face with our own experience and set working in that experience the leaven of the highest culture. For it is exalted desires that give their validity to revolutions. . . .

For Van Wyck Brooks, and for the decade generally, the soul of man under socialism seemed more likely to fulfill the Jeffersonian ideal of the spirit than the soul of man under the industrial order of 1918.

Van Wyck Brooks, however, has burned what he once adored, and now adores what once he burned, and posterity has forgotten the name of James Oppenheim. If we seek for a central figure who, like Willa Cather in the case of the fascination of art for youth, and, like William Vaughn Moody in the case of the fascination of myth for youth, shall embody for us the revolt of youth in the direction of social radicalism, we shall find, I think, that the more we study the situation, the more we are haunted by the radiant, half-forgotten figure of Randolph Bourne. I say "half-forgotten," knowing that he receives sympathetic treatment in Alfred Kazin's admirable history of twentieth-century prose, and in one or two other places. Yet the erudite *Literary History of the United States* gives him small space and smaller sympathy, and the brief discussion therein contained ends with the appalling sentence: "In a blind search for values in a distorted world, he died." The world may be distorted, but I cannot agree that Bourne's search for values was blind, nor was he the unintelligent rebel the passage seems to imply.

When Randolph Bourne died December 22, 1918, a victim of the influenza epidemic, *The New Republic,*

The Dial, and other liberal magazines regretfully chron-
icled the passing of a figure who had already become
legendary. He was, said Oppenheim in a memorial
poem, the "imperishable symbol of our ongoing." In
the volume memorializing his contemporary, Paul
Rosenfeld, Bourne appears as "the soul of a generation,"
that "figure in a black cape, almost Gothic in his
chiseled look," "who despite his hunchback, seemed the
tallest figure" Rosenfeld had ever seen, "Bourne, the
one time piano shop employee who somehow suggested
a high-tuned instrument," "Bourne standing indomi-
tably, in his . . . student's cape, as the personification
of all that was vital and brave and good." He died
almost in Rosenfeld's presence, and his passing was
characteristic: after a "muttered request for a glass of
eggnog," he exclaimed "at the glory of its golden tint
as the light of the morning sun illuminated the tumbler,"
then collapsed in the arms of his nurse. For Rosenfeld,
"a large and amazing intelligence had gone out of the
world." Edward Sapir wrote from Canada to pay
tribute to the "keen edge of a remorseless sincerity," and
in *The New Republic* Floyd Dell summed him up by
saying that he "belonged to us, and stood for us,"
meaning the generation in social revolt. In him the
rebellion of youth, particularly its social radicalism, was
"clarified and transfigured," and Dell continues:

He was of us, because he had a restless and relentless
curiosity, undeterred by sentiment and never recoiling in
cynicism; the mood of perpetual inquiry, and the courage to

go down unfamiliar ways in search of truth. These are traits of our generation; but in many of us they show themselves for the most part as anxious hopes and stubborn fears, violent and apparently perverse disloyalties to accustomed ideals, wanton or whimsical followings of private and inexplicable fancy. In literature, in art, in politics, in all departments of life, there has been an alienation of the younger generation from traditional mode of action.

Randolph Bourne was born in Bloomfield, New Jersey, May 30, 1886. A fall in infancy permanently disfigured him, dowering him with a hunched back, a stunted body, and an enormous head. Nevertheless, as Van Wyck Brooks was to write,

one divined him in a moment, the fine mettlesome temper of his intellect, his curiosity, his acutely critical self-consciousness, his aesthetic flair, his delicate sense of personal relationships, his toughness of fibre, his masterly powers of assimilation, his grasp of reality, his burning convictions, his beautifully precise desires.

He attended the New Jersey public schools and entered Columbia University in 1909, graduating four years later, and acquiring at that time the Gilder Fellowship, which permitted him a year of European travel, and produced a masterly report on Europe as it was before World War I. Already he had begun to contribute to the *Atlantic Monthly* a series of essays, cumulated in book form as *Youth and Life,* published the year of his graduation (1913), the first of five such collections. The war turned him into a sceptic, and he remained a pacifist. An essay entitled "The War and the Intellectuals," contributed to *The Seven Arts* in June, 1917, is a searing indictment of the flaccidity of Americans in succumbing to war hysteria. Another essay, "Twilight of the Idols," in the October number, bade farewell to John Dewey, whose disciple Bourne had been. But Bourne could not join Dewey in plumping for war. Having surveyed the youthful drafted soldiers, he wrote in July, 1917: "If the enterprise goes on endlessly, the work, so blithely undertaken for the defence of democracy, will have crushed out the only genuinely precious thing in a nation, the hope and ardent idealism of its youth." The government clamped down on *The Masses,* for which Bourne had been writing. *The Seven Arts* failed, and Bourne's last months were not merely a period of poverty, they were a period in which it was difficult for him to print anything. Nevertheless, this cripple remains the best philosopher of radicalism in American art.

In his volume, *The History of a Literary Radical,* and in other essays on education, Bourne shows how the inadequate American education of his generation had turned him into a rebel. His apostasy began with the study of English literature in college, an experience which, if it did not deprive him of his cultural loyalty, at any rate deadened his appetite for the genteel. He thus describes the introductory course: He

was given a huge anthology, a sort of press-clipping bureau of *belles-lettres,* from Chaucer to Arthur Symons. Under the

direction of a professor who was laying out a career for himself as a poet — or "modern singer," as he expressed it — the
class went briskly through the centuries, sampling their
genius and tasting the various literary flavors. The enterprise
reminded [him] of those books of woollen samples which one
looks through when one is to have a suit of clothes made.
. . . All that was expected of him, apparently, was that he
should become familiar, from these microscopic pieces, with
the different textures and patterns. . . . There was not time
for preferences. Indeed the professor strove diligently to give
each writer his just due. How was one to appreciate the
great thoughts and the great styles if one began to choose
violently between them, or attempt any discrimination on
grounds of their peculiar congeniality for one's own soul?
Criticism had to spurn such subjectivity, scholarship could
not be willful. The neatly arranged book of "readings," with
its medicinal doses of inspiration, became the symbol of [his]
education.

In an article in *The New Republic* for 1916 Bourne was
to plead for an education that would lead to "a liberation of taste from the sterile control of the 'best.'"
"Indigenous style," he then said, "is the only style that
means anything."

The mechanical righteousness of the survey course,
that last manifestation of traditional humanism, seemed
to Bourne symbolical. It stood for the entire value system arranged by the elder generation, and to the
destruction of that system he devoted his essays, especially those in *Youth and Life* and in *The History of a
Literary Radical*. The elder generation, he roundly
declared, displays a "gradual losing of the grip of life,

a slow withdrawing into an ideal world of phrases," and when one's elders warn youth to take lessons from experience, they really refer to a slow accretion of inhibitions. The capitalist order, he said, is "run by these damaged ideals." In *Youth and Life* he examined this notion with indignant clarity. Youth, he said, profoundly doubts "the old rigid morality, with its emphasis on the prudential virtues," the neglect of "the fundamental fact" of man's irrationality. The family, the professions, business, and industry are mainly sentimental bonds, forged to keep the young in line.

He revolted against the industrial order because it seemed to him to stifle the individualism that Croly was trying to protect in *The Promise of American Life*. Business offered only an insoluble dilemma. The industrial world presented no incentive to individual responsibility. Merely to avoid these pressures is "to have gone a long way towards guaranteeing one's real success," and success for him was releasing the great, rich rush and flood of youthful energy. Youth he defined as the period for giving full play to good impulses rather than merely checking bad ones, and he applauded the instinct in youth which sees the adventure of life as a tonic and a spur, and suggested that, by adapting the device of Socratic irony, youth could hold at bay the hounds of the bitch goddess, Success.

Bourne's rebellion was not merely emotional. He talked of self-expression, but he was too intelligent to believe that mere self-expression is a program. He refused negativism as a theory of government — that negative laissez-faire philosophy which had satisfied William Graham Sumner and Andrew Carnegie. The charm of socialism to "so many of the rising generation," he wrote, lies in its positive, scientific spirit, its claim to historical basis, its definite organization for the attainment of social ends. Youth is being converted to the possibilities of a regenerated American society, to which it is led by the insight of art and by its own fresh vitality, and he thought the appeal of socialism lay just there, the appeal

to our delight in a healthy, free, social life, to an artistic longing for a society where the treasures of civilization may be open to all, and to our desire for an environment where we ourselves will be able to exercise our capacities, and exert the untrammeled influences which we believe might be ours and our fellows.

And in turning, grief-stricken, away from John Dewey, who was his idol and who had declared that the intellectuals must support the war against Germany, Bourne did so in the belief that the duty of youth, and of youth in art, should "take the form of a heightened energy and enthusiasm for life in the midst of a world of death."

Here, I think, is *par excellence* the philosopher of youthful American radicalism, of a generation in revolt. For that generation Bourne helped to create a program of ideas. Morality was to spring forth, not under the outer sanctions of duty, but under the inner sanctions of virtue. Life was to be lived in the United States for its own sake, not as a preparation for dying. The touchstone of education, of religion, of politics was to be joy rather than obedience. He did not repudiate religion, but he held that religion had little to do with mere activism, since, as he wrote, "to be religious is to turn our gaze away from the dynamic to the static and the permanent," — an unfortunate statement, since all he was trying to do was to rescue religion from the nineteenth century. In that endeavor he ventured on the paradox that religion has only a secondary relation to ethics: "We have no right to demand that it operate practically, nor can we call altruistic activity, and enthusiasm for a noble cause, religion." In short, he was not deceived by the social gospel, though he held that there were permanent ends not being served by the industrial system.

Therefore it seemed to him that a sterile worship of the American past was stultifying the creation of a rich American present. For him, a radical transformation was necessary — a transformation that might turn the republic into a socialist state, but it was to be an American socialist state, owing nothing to Marx, whom he indignantly repudiated, and nothing to Europe, but everything to the dream of the founding fathers. It is a comment on Bourne that books like *The Naked and the Dead* and *From Here to Eternity* show that he was right in more ways than it is comfortable to realize, wherein we watch frustrations originally felt by the young artist only, extend themselves to take in the ordinary young American, as Bourne prophesied they would.

Whether one accepts Bourne's goal of an American socialist state is less important than is an understanding of the significance of his point of view. That point of view is the point of view of an American radicalism, and I think something precious and sanative has passed out of American writing with the vanishing of the one form of literary radicalism which, as our literary history demonstrates, has enduring value. Part of a poem by Witter Bynner laconically expresses the attitude I am struggling to define:

> Said the old men to the young men:
>   "It is finished — you may go!"
> Said the young men to the old men:
>   "No."
>
> Said the old men to the young men:
>   "What is there more to do?"
> Said the young men to the old men:
>   "You."

It is not thus that Europe traditionally speaks.

The fascination of the bright Medusa for youth has been sometimes destructive or fallacious, as I have tried to demonstrate, but in so far as American writing has learned to refresh itself by perpetually recurring to the Utopian ideals and cultural theory which created the republic, that fascination has been justified by its products. The life of art is fruitful only within the framework of civic virtue, as works from *Antigone* to

Faust redundantly demonstrate. If the equality of individuals and the dignity of man be myths, they are myths to which the republic is committed, and they justify Archibald MacLeish in his famous demand that we restore the man of letters to his essential and historic place in democratic society. What is sound and sweet in the revolt of youth is something more than postwar rebellion or modern cynicism, it is that power of passionate honesty which demands that the state shall trust its citizens and not fear them. The state ought not to be that great leviathan, before whom the free soul is compelled to bow down. The virtue of youth in art as it is the virtue of youth in life is sincerely to put the right questions and passionately to keep on demanding the right answers until they are given. The note of radicalism is, in this view, a republican and individual note which cannot be too often sounded. Otherwise we drift into the gloomy future prophesied for us by, for example, Aldous Huxley in *Brave New World*.

I cannot do better in concluding these lectures than to quote the remarkable paragraph with which my colleague, Professor Albert Guerard, ends his penetrating *André Gide*, published by Harvard University Press in 1951. When, after pointing out that, amid all his tergiversations, Gide is fundamentally and always a moralist, Mr. Guerard says:

Since 1947 the pressure of events has more and more forced upon us — upon education as well as government — the expedient decision and convenient fiction, the virtuous rationalization of impulses to power or survival, the collective hypnotic illusion. We have become pragmatists on a monstrous scale, and are much closer than most people think to the world of Orwell's 1984, where what ought to be is "honestly" mistaken for what is. The pragmatist's truth . . . has gradually come to seem more true than fact. The mechanisms of propaganda grow constantly more powerful, and with them our capacities for self-flattery and self-delusion. It is hard to see how, in the years that face us, young people will learn to think truthfully, rather than to think usefully or patriotically. In such a world, we can be sure, there will be few demoralizers to combat the radio, the newspaper, the communiqué, the leaflet. These few may seem merely decadent, and Gide himself the product of a dead culture and leisure class. Yet perhaps only these few demoralizers will save us.

I suggest that the revolt of youth in the name of art, despite its weaknesses which I have tried patiently to explore, was in its day, in Mr. Guerard's sense, a healthy movement of demoralization, and I, for one, hope that youth will again revolt and again demoralize the dead weight of conformity that now lies upon us.